W9-BEA-727

LIBRARY
LYNDHURST HIGH SCHO
LYNDHURST, N. J.

CHINA

Peggy Ferroa

MARSHALL CAVENDISH
New York • London • Sydney

Editorial Director	Shirley Hew
Managing Editor	Shova Loh
Editors	Goh Sui Noi
	Leonard Lau
	Roseline Lum
	Siow Peng Han
	Tan Kok Eng
	MaryLee Knowlton
Picture Editor	Y.M. Kaung
Production	Edmund Lam
Art Manager	Tuck Loong
Design	Ang Siew Lian
	Lee Woon Hong
	Ong Su Ping
	Katherine Tan
Illustrators	Kelvin Sim
	Cherine Lim
Cover picture	Bernard Sonneville

Reference edition published 1991 by
Marshall Cavendish Corporation
2415 Jerusalem Avenue
North Bellmore
N.Y. 11710

Printed in Singapore by Times Offset Pte Ltd

All rights reserved. No part of this book may be reproduced or utilized in any form or by any means electronic or mechanical, including photocopying, recording, or by an information storage and retrieval system, without permission from the copyright holder.

© Times Editions Pte Ltd 1991

Originated and designed by
Times Books International
an imprint of Times Editions Pte Ltd
Times Center, 1 New Industrial Road
Singapore 1953
Telex: 37908 EDTIME Fax: 2854871

Library of Congress Cataloging-in-Publication Data:
Ferroa, Peggy Grace, 1959–
    China / Peggy Grace Ferroa.—Reference ed.
      p. cm.—(Cultures of the World)
    Includes bibliographical references and index.
      Summary: A look at the geography, history, government, economy, people, lifestyles, religion, language, and culture of the world's most populous nation.
    ISBN 1–85435–399–3
    1. China—Juvenile literature. [1. China.]
I. Title. II. Series.
DS706.F38 1991
951—dc20   91–15865
                      CIP
                      AC

INTRODUCTION

China was home to one of the most ancient civilizations in the world, where the "son of heaven," the emperor, reigned supreme. It was the "Mysterious East," not easily accessible to the outside world because it was bordered by inhospitable mountains and deserts. The first known route to China from the West was overland through treacherous deserts, the Silk Road, through which merchants arrived on their camel caravans, seeking silks, teas and other exotic oriental goods.

In 1949, China became the People's Republic of China, under the Communist regime led by Mao Zedong. The world turned its back on China and it, in turn, closed its doors to the outside world. With the death of Mao, China underwent a series of reforms, which opened it to the rest of the world once again.

In this book, part of the series *Cultures of the World*, we take a peek behind the Bamboo Curtain into a world where a socialist country lives in constant reminder of its Chinese heritage.

BEIJING

CONTENTS

Playing elephant chess, a favorite pastime among the Chinese.

CONTENTS

Women in China work side by side with men, in the fields, in government, in large organizations. Men share responsibilities with women in the home.

GEOGRAPHY

THE MIDDLE KINGDOM, as China is known to the Chinese, sits in the eastern part of Asia, and covers an area of 3.7 million square miles. It is the third largest country in the world and is slightly larger than the United States of America.

China shares its border with 12 countries. To its north is Mongolia, to its east, North Korea, and to its northeast and northwest, the Soviet Union. Afghanistan, Pakistan, India, Nepal, Sikkim and Bhutan lie to the west and southwest and to its south are Myanmar, Laos and Vietnam. Its coastline is bounded by the Bohai, Yellow, East and South China seas.

China's land mass is made up mainly of mountains, plateaus and deserts. Of its total land mass, only 10% can be used to cultivate food to feed 1.2 billion people. It is, therefore, a feat that China grows enough to feed its own people and to export to other countries.

Stretching 3,420 miles from north to south, China's climate ranges from cruel Siberian frosts, to mild temperate, to lush tropical weather. Although China straddles four time zones, the whole country follows the same time as that of its capital, Beijing.

Below: **China and its neighbors.**

Opposite: **A hillside farming village.**

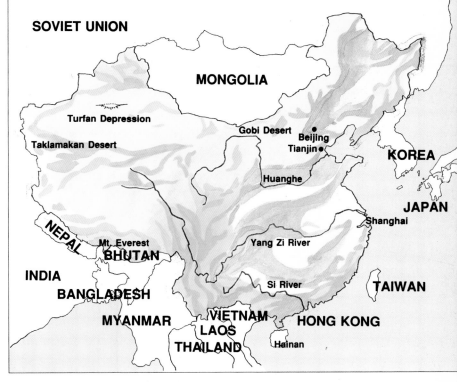

The unusually shaped hills of Guilin, Guangxi, in southwest China, are a favorite subject of Chinese painters.

TERRAIN

China's varied terrain includes every geographical formation imaginable. Starting from the west, we find the highest plateau on earth—Tibet. At over 13,500 feet above sea level, it is no wonder that it is called the "Roof of The World." Just south of this plateau is the Himalayan mountain range. Mount Everest, or Qomolangma Feng, as it is known to the Chinese, sits on the China-Nepal border.

Moving north from the plateau, the terrain drops to between 3,280 and 6,560 feet above sea level. Here we find the famous grasslands of Mongolia, important to cattle breeding, and the Gobi Desert.

In the northwest of China, we find the Taklamakan Desert, the largest in China through which the ancient Silk Road passed. Nearby, bordered by the Tian mountains, is the Turfan Depression. Known as the "Oasis of Fire," it is the hottest spot in China with temperatures reaching 120 F.

In central China is the Yang Zi river delta, an important agricultural area and heavily populated. Going further south, the geography changes more dramatically, with unusually shaped cliffs, gorges and waterfalls.

8

CLIMATE

China's climate is as varied as its terrain. Inhabitants in the north live with severe, bitterly cold winters. In the northernmost part, temperatures can drop to -18 F. In the northern city of Harbin, for example, it is so cold that every winter sees an exhibition of ice sculptures. In the Yang Zi river delta, the weather is warm and humid with four distinct seasons. Winters are much shorter, with the temperature around 32 F.

Parts of the country, such as Mongolia in the north and Xinjiang in the northwest, experience extreme weather conditions within a single day. It can start off freezing cold in the morning and by midday, it will be boiling hot. This is because the terrain is varied and desert covers large areas.

Winter in Beijing, the capital of China. Winter days in northern China are sunny, dry—and cold.

China is officially divided into North and South by the Yang Zi River. Taking for granted that the South is warmer than the North, cities south of the river are not entitled to central heating in their buildings. During winter, it is not surprising to find residents of cities just south of the river bundled up like Eskimos indoors.

Summers in the North can be as punishing as the winters. Temperatures can reach highs of 100 F or more. It can get just as hot in summer in the South and even more uncomfortable because the higher humidity makes one sweaty. The best weather to be had is in autumn, when it is cool and dry. Spring in the North brings sand storms from Mongolia and it is hard to keep the fine sand out of the tiniest cracks in homes.

The Yang Zi, or Chang-jiang. Because of its length, of which 1,700 miles are navigable, it is China's main waterway, linking inland and sea-ports and major cities. Large ships can travel as far as Wuhan, 700 miles upriver from the coast.

WATERWAYS

YANG ZI RIVER It is also known as Changjiang, or "Long River." Its source in the Qinghai-Tibetan mountains, the Yang Zi is the longest river in China and the third longest in the world, measuring 3,915 miles. It flows through nine provinces, Qinghai, Tibet, Sichuan, Yunnan, Hubei, Hunan, Jiangxi, Anhui and Jiangsu, emptying into the East China Sea near Shanghai.

The Yang Zi officially divides China into the North and South. It has 700 tributaries and flows through important industrial areas. The Yang Zi river delta is also agriculturally important. Here is where half of China's crops are grown and where the fields grow most of China's staple, rice.

THE HUANGHE The Huanghe, or Yellow River, starts as melting snow in the Qinghai-Tibetan mountains. Its journey of 3,395 miles passes through nine provinces. It empties into the Bohai Sea. As it flows through the Central Chinese Loess Plateau, it picks up an incredible amount of silt. This loose yellow soil is what gives the river its name, and the

THE GRAND CANAL

The Grand Canal is the oldest and longest man-made canal in China, if not the world. First dug 2,000 years ago, this project was as immense as the Great Wall in terms of labor and lives lost. It is 1,114 miles long and was first built during the 4th century B.C. to link the then capital of Luoyang to the old capital of Xian. It was gradually extended over the years by various emperors to join Hangzhou in the south

and Beijing in the north. The main purpose of this canal was to mobilize troops in times of war, but it became used mostly to transport food from the fertile South to the barren North. This gradually made the South the agricultural center of China.

The Grand Canal connects four major rivers—the Huanghe, Yang Zi, Huai and Qiantang. It passes through some of the prettiest parts of China such as Suzhou and Hangzhou.

Much of the canal has fallen into disuse due to road and railway links and the flooding of the Huanghe. Now, only one-third of the original canal is in use, mainly to transport agricultural products and raw materials to factories and warehouses. It is also used to irrigate the drought-prone areas of Hubei, Henan and Anhui.

problems it causes give the river another name, "China's Sorrow."

One billion tons of silt are carried downstream each year, making the Huanghe the muddiest river in the world. The amount of silt it deposits can add 12 miles of land around the coast in three years. The riverbed is raised by four inches annually, causing the river banks to flood. The river has changed its course 12 times over the centuries because of this silt buildup. Near its estuary, the water is so thick and low there is little marine activity.

The Huanghe is also known as the "Cradle of Chinese Civilization." Loess is very fertile earth and it was along the banks of this river that the Hans first started to cultivate land. Consequently, villages and empires grew.

Beijingers on their "metal horses," the main mode of transportation in Chinese cities.

CITIES

BEIJING Beijing is China's capital. It has been in existence for eight centuries and is one of the oldest and best known cities in the world, containing some of the finest buildings and palaces.

In the center of Beijing is Tiananmen Square, or "The Gate of Heavenly Peace." The largest public square in the world, it can hold up to 1 million people at any one time. It was here that on October 1, 1949, Chairman Mao Zedong proclaimed the founding of the People's Republic of China. The gate itself, Tiananmen, was once used as the main gate to the Ming and Qing imperial palaces and today visitors still use this gate as entrance to the Forbidden City. During the Qing dynasty, the square was enclosed by a red wall and commoners only entered it for execution.

With a population of 10.8 million people, this bustling commercial city with its numerous foreign embassies is also the seat of government. It is here that China's 23 provinces, five autonomous regions and three municipalities are looked after.

FORBIDDEN CITY

Perhaps the most famous complex of buildings in Beijing, if not China, is the Forbidden City. It is so called because it was forbidden to all except those who were living there. This cluster of imperial palaces was built in A.D. 1406–20 during the Ming dynasty. It is surrounded by a wide moat and a high wall. In all, it has 9,999 rooms and it has been estimated that if a newborn baby lived in one room every day of his life, he would be 27 years old by the time he was through with them.

The area around the Forbidden City is equally interesting. Medieval buildings once catering to the needs of the nearby palaces are still standing. In fact, the imperial pharmacy today still dispenses the same kind of pills and potions that used to cure princes, and the royal shoe shop is not far off.

SHANGHAI Shanghai sits at the meeting point of two rivers, the Huangpu and Wusong. It has always been an important port in China and today it handles the country's largest amount of freight annually.

In the mid-19th century, after the Opium Wars, it became an international concession and opened its doors to the West. Foreign banks, shops and embassies were built, all with a distinct European flavor. Shanghainese were exposed to a more Western lifestyle and thought themselves more sophisticated than their fellow Chinese elsewhere. Shanghai was once called the "Paris of the East" and shadows of that racy era still loom in the old buildings.

Shanghainese live in China's most populous city with 13 million inhabitants. Within the city area alone, there are about 19,000 living in a square mile. It is so crowded that not every one gets a day off on the same day. They have to take turns as the narrow streets and public transportation system cannot handle the large number of people otherwise.

A busy street in Guangzhou. At the turn of the century, Guangzhou was a center for anti-imperial and revolutionary movements.

GUANGZHOU Guangzhou, or Canton, is the capital of Guangdong province. Guangzhou is one of the most ancient of Chinese cities with a history that goes back 20 centuries. Legend has it that five gods came riding into the city on five rams. Each brought a six-eared rice plant so that the town would forever be free of famine. They vanished while the rams turned into stone. There is a sculpture of five rams in the town and Guangzhou is still known as the "City of Rams."

Guangzhou sits on the fertile delta of the Zhujiang or Pearl River, facing the South China Sea. Because of its position, it was visited by Indian and Roman merchants as far back as the 2nd century A.D. It is now an important trade and industrial city.

Cantonese, the local dialect, is commonly spoken here. Being far south of China, its weather is warm and moist almost all year round. It has lush, green vegetation, abundant rice fields and fruit orchards.

Over 5 million people live in this vibrant city which is one of the most modern and enterprising places in China.

FLORA AND FAUNA

China's plant life includes nearly all species of plants found in the frigid and temperate regions. Plants dating back to the Ice Age have been found untouched in some hidden corners of the country. Its forests are filled with cypresses, pine and bamboo. A large variety of flowers can also be found. There are hundreds of varieties of chrysanthemums and peonies that can grow to the size of a child's head.

China's range of wildlife is just as large. There are over 100 species of rare endangered animals, including the giant panda, golden monkey and Manchurian tiger.

THE GIANT PANDA

The giant panda, China's favorite animal, is threatened with extinction. Pandas live only on a diet of bamboo leaves. With urbanization, more and more bamboo plants are destroyed, forcing the animals to go higher up into the mountains in search of food. To make matters worse, the bamboo has a very slow growth cycle. Some species can take up to 100 years to grow. Most pandas die of starvation due to the shrinking bamboo forests.

Pandas are found in the regions of Sichuan, Shaanxi and Gansu provinces. About 1,000 pandas are known to be living in their natural habitat.

HISTORY

THERE IS EVIDENCE that primitive man lived in China some 400,000 to 500,000 years ago. In December 1929 the first complete skull of the 690,000-year-old Peking Man was discovered in a limestone cave not far from Beijing. The cradle of Chinese civilization is said to be the Yellow River (Huanghe).

EARLY HISTORY

Chinese consider the time before the 21st century B.C. the legendary period. This was a time where fact and fiction mingled—a time when rulers were immortal and dragons and mythical creatures prowled the earth. One of these mythical creatures became human and founded the Xia dynasty, which ruled from 2205 to 1766 B.C. It is not certain whether this dynasty ever existed, but evidence has been found on the dynasty that followed, the Shang (1766–1123 B.C.).

Opposite: **The Monument to the People's Heroes on Tiananmen Square in Beijing.**

CHRONOLOGICAL HISTORY

Legendary Period	pre–21st century B.C.	Sui Dynasty	581–618
Xia Dynasty	2205–1766 B.C.	Tang Dynasty	618–907
Shang Dynasty	1766–1123 B.C.	Five Dynasties	907–960
Western Zhou Dynasty	1122–770 B.C.	Northern Song Dynasty	960–1127
Eastern Zhou Dynasty		Southern Song Dynasty	1127–1279
Spring and Autumn Period	770–476 B.C.	Liao Dynasty	907–1125
Warring States Period	475–221 B.C.	Western Xia Dynasty	1032–1227
Qin Dynasty	221–206 B.C.	Jin Dynasty	1115–1234
Western Han Dynasty	206 B.C.–A.D.24	Yuan Dynasty (Mongolian)	1271–1368
Eastern Han Dynasty	25–220	Ming Dynasty	1368–1644
The Three Kingdoms	220–316	Qing Dynasty (Manchurian)	1644–1911
Western Jin Dynasty	265–316	Republic of China	1912–1949
Eastern Jin Dynasty	317–420	People's Republic of China	1949 to present
Northern And Southern Dynasties	420–589		

A wall mural depicting a scene from the Spring and Autumn period, a time of disorder and chaos as feudal states fought each other for power.

Urban societies existed during the Shang dynasty and records of daily life and literature have been found carved on bone, tortoise shells and bronze, as paper had not yet been invented.

The Shangs were conquered by the Zhous who ruled by a feudal system, that is, leaders of the different states of the empire swore loyalty and paid taxes to the emperor. The discovery of iron casting during this period helped in the making of farming tools and irrigation was developed on a large scale. China became one of the most advanced areas in the world at that time. It was also during this time that Chinese philosophies such as Taoism and Confucianism evolved, making their mark on Chinese thinking until the present day.

After 200 years of peace, the Zhou dynasty disintegrated into smaller squabbling states (Spring and Autumn period) which later grouped into larger states (Warring States period).

QIN SHIHUANG

China was truly united for the first time under Qin Shihuang, or "the first exalted emperor." He ascended the throne of the state of Qin at the age of 13 and went on to conquer its surrounding states. He completed conquest of the other states in 221 B.C. Although his reign lasted only 35 years or so, he will always be remembered for the great and terrible things he did.

Qin Shihuang abolished the feudal system and established a new order of society that was to remain in China for the next 2,000 years. People were divided into different classes. There were aristocrats, landowners, bureaucrats, peasants, merchants and slaves.

Qin Shihuang set up a central government. An imperial examination was started to recruit the best scholars as civil servants. The examination system stressed the importance of learning. This raised the level of education and culture and made China a nation of scholars.

Qin Shihuang standardized the written language. He also established a system of weights and measures and a form of currency. Communication links to the capital, such as roads and canals, were set up.

A shrewd and jealous man, Qin Shihuang was well-known for his tyranny. It is said that he burned alive hundreds of scholars if their views were different from his or if they appeared smarter than he. He also burned thousands of books for the same reason. Precious works of great teachers such as Confucius and Mencius were destroyed and what we read now were rewritten by scholars from memory.

In 1974, farmers digging for a well in Xian came across one of the most important discoveries of history—a vault containing 6,000 terracotta warriors in full uniform and battle formation protecting Qin Shihuang's nearby tomb.

Records show that the tomb of Qin Shihuang is beautiful. Its ceiling is said to be studded with pearls and gems to represent the moon, sun and stars. Birds and animals of precious material sit in emerald pine forests and mercury flows to simulate rivers.

THE GREAT WALL

The Great Wall stretches for 4,160 miles across North China. It is the only man-made structure that can be seen from the moon with the naked eye. Its construction started as far back as the Spring and Autumn period (770–476 B.C.) and the Warring States period (475–221 B.C.). Rival feudal kingdoms built walls around their territories to keep out invading nomadic tribes from the north. When Qin Shihuang unified China, he started to link up and extend these walls.

Prisoners of war, convicts, soldiers, civilians and farmers provided the labor. Millions died for this cause and many Chinese stories speak of parted lovers and men dying of starvation and disease. Their bodies were buried in the foundations of the wall or used to make up its thickness.

The Great Wall crosses loess plateaus, mountains, deserts, rivers and valleys, passing through five provinces and two autonomous regions. It is about 20 feet wide and 26 feet high. Parts of the wall are so broad that 10 soldiers can walk abreast. Materials used were whatever could be found near by—clay, stone, willow branches, reeds and sand.

Parts of this wall can still be seen in remote parts of China. What most visitors see of the Wall now was restored in the Ming dynasty, when stone slabs replaced clay bricks. It took 100 years to rebuild and it is said that the amount of material used in the present wall alone is enough to circle the world at the equator five times.

HAN DYNASTY

Over the centuries, China was ruled for the most time by dynasties. Emperors usually passed down their title to male heirs. A dynasty can last decades or even centuries. Perhaps the two most important dynasties in Chinese history were the Han and Tang.

The Han dynasty (206 B.C.–A.D. 220) was established after the overthrow of Qin Shihuang. It made such an impression on China that, even today, the Chinese refer to themselves as "Men of Han."

During the Han dynasty, the Chinese empire stretched from the Pamirs (mountains in today's Afghanistan) in the west to Korea in the east, and from Mongolia in the north to Vietnam in the south. During this time, the Silk Road became well traveled and contacts were made with Central and Western Asia, and even with Rome. Trade flourished and China was opened to other cultures.

Buddhism was introduced from India and Confucianism became the state doctrine. Knowledge of Confucian Classics became essential for officials and candidates for the civil service. Developments were made in painting and the arts and many historical and philosophical works were written.

During the Han dynasty, a new style of writing was developed, which was suited to the compilation of official documents. The first Chinese dictionary was put together in A.D. 100; it contained 9,000 words with explanations of their meanings and the different forms used in writing.

There was advancement in science and technology. Water clocks and sundials were used by officials so they could complete their work on time. Paper was discovered and a seismograph developed.

The Han dynasty lasted 400 years but corrupt and weak rulers led to its downfall.

The Han dynasty was founded by Liu Bang, a peasant-rebel who once urinated into the hat of a court scholar to show his disdain for education. However, he later proved himself a practical and flexible ruler when he had learned men in his court.

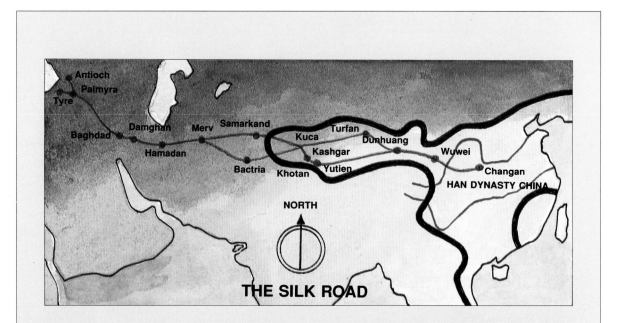

THE SILK ROAD

The ancient Silk Road was established some 2,000 years ago. It started at the Han capital of Changan (today's Xian) and stretched west for 4,350 miles. Crossing mountains and deserts, it branched into two routes, one going through Central and Western Asia to the eastern shore of the Mediterranean, the other crossing the Aral and Caspian Seas to Constantinople. From here, silk was carried on to Rome and Venice.

Chinese silk and the four great inventions of China, paper, printing, gunpowder and the compass, made its way to the rest of Asia and to Europe along this route. In return, merchants brought religion, and the art and culture of these foreign regions to China. They also brought agricultural products and the Chinese soon began eating grapes, walnuts, cucumbers, broad beans and watermelon. Silk was also exchanged for Persian horses, glass, perfume and ivory.

Merchants traveled the Silk Road on camels. Chosen because of their docile temper and their endurance to the sun and sand, these animals carried goods, merchants, homes and musicians across mountains and deserts. Few persons traveled the entire Road. Goods passed from middlemen to middlemen at various junctions along the Road.

Later, with the loss of Roman territory in Asia, the Silk Road became unsafe and few people traveled it. In the 13th and 14th centuries, the Mongols who then ruled China revived use of the Road. It was through the Silk Road that Marco Polo, the Italian merchant-adventurer, arrived in Mongol-ruled China.

TANG DYNASTY

The next 400 years saw China divided into separate kingdoms constantly fighting for power. The nomadic tribes from the north were also trying to get a foothold in China and, for a while, succeeded. Four dynasties followed the Han dynasty—the Western Jin, Eastern Jin, Northern and Southern dynasties, and the Sui. The Sui dynasty went bankrupt because large expansion programs in public works and expeditions to Central Asia drained the country of money. However, the Suis laid the groundwork for one of the most famous Chinese dynasties, the Tang dynasty. The Tang family, who were related to the Suis, led China into the Golden Age of Chinese history.

A wall mural showing Tang court maids.

The Tang dynasty lasted from A.D. 618 to 907, during which Central Asia, Korea and northern Vietnam came under China's rule. Developments were made in agriculture and farming tools, increasing food production. The country's administration was run by the best scholars well-schooled in Confucianism. Chinese arts and literature flourished and the art of printing arose.

Tang rule gradually deteriorated and was overthrown by the Songs. No other dynasty had such an effect on China as the Tang. Many of the dynasties that followed modeled themselves on the Tang dynasty in the hope of achieving the same heights of glory. Unfortunately, none did.

THE FOUR GREAT INVENTIONS OF ANCIENT CHINA

Many things that we take for granted in our everyday life were invented in China. For example, the umbrella, eyeglasses, paper money, kites, the mechanical clock and the washboard made their way to the West after years of being used in China. The most important four inventions from ancient China are paper, printing, gunpowder and the compass.

PAPER Before paper was invented, the Chinese carved characters on bone and tortoise shell. Later, the first book was bound using strips of bamboo held together with string. People then started writing on silk, which proved too expensive. Paper first made its appearance in the Han dynasty (206 B.C.–A.D. 220). Bark, bits of hemp, cloth and old fishing nets were boiled, rinsed, pounded and stretched out on fine bamboo screens.

PRINTING At first printing blocks each contained one page of text. This meant that each block could only be used to produce the same page of a book. During the Song dynasty (A.D. 960–1279), single words were engraved on individual blocks of wood. Words could now be used over and over again. Words were inked and moistened paper placed over them. Up to 600 books containing 60,000 words could be printed in a month.

GUNPOWDER During the period of the Warring States (403–221 B.C.), gunpowder was discovered accidentally by alchemists trying to make immortality pills. A mixture of sulphur and saltpeter caused an explosion when heated. It was first used in war during the Tang dynasty (A.D. 618–907).

COMPASS The compass was first used more than 2,000 years ago when the Chinese discovered that a piece of natural magnetite would automatically point to a north-south direction. The Chinese soon started to fashion magnets of ingenious designs. One was of a wooden figure on a horse-drawn chariot and no matter which direction the chariot turned, the figure would always be pointing north. Compasses soon came into use in navigation and opened up the world to China.

THE LAST DYNASTY

China came under imperial rule for the last time in 1644 when the Ming dynasty was overthrown by Manchurians from the north. The Qing dynasty ruled for over 200 years during which their territory included Manchuria, Mongolia, Tibet, Taiwan and Turkestan (Xinjiang). It was larger than the empire had ever been. For the first 150 years, the country was well-run and prospered under able emperors. This soon gave way to power struggles of corrupt court officials.

The Summer Palace built by Empress Cixi of the Qing dynasty in 1873. She took money meant for the modernization of the navy to build the palace. This and other misuse of money, together with other events, led to the weakening and eventual collapse of the Qing dynasty.

Few Europeans saw China as only Canton (Guangzhou) was open to them. The Europeans came to buy Chinese goods such as tea, silk and porcelain. But they could not sell anything to China which was largely self-sufficient. In order to balance the trade, the British started selling opium to the Chinese. The Qing government tried to ban its sale, but corrupt officials and merchants did nothing to stop it. This soon led to a series of wars known as the Opium Wars, in which the Chinese lost.

The Qing government submitted to the British by signing the Treaty of Nanjing. This meant that the British were given land which became British territory, or concession, and could open ports. Hong Kong became a British colony. Other European nations forced the government to sign similar treaties.

China was soon in debt and its people were heavily taxed. Soon, the Taiping Rebellion broke out in the south. This weakened the Manchus even more, as Britain, France and Russia took the opportunity to occupy even more Chinese land. The Qing dynasty finally collapsed in 1911.

LIBRARY
LYNDHURST HIGH SCHOOL
LYNDHURST, N. J.

A statue of Sun Yat-sen in Jiangsu province. Sun is known as the father of modern China.

Opposite: **A portrait of Mao Zedong at Tiananmen. Inspired by the ideals of Sun Yat-sen, he joined the revolutionary army in 1911. He later led the Communist Party to victory against the Kuomintang in 1949.**

MODERN CHINA

Sun Yat-sen, leader of the Kuomintang (National People's Party) established the Republic of China in 1911 and became its president. China, however, was not at peace as warlords in various parts of China fought for power. One in particular, Yuan Shi Kai, a former Qing minister, controlled much of northern China. In order to keep peace, Sun gave up the presidency to Yuan.

Yuan declared himself emperor in 1912 and made Beijing his capital. He died after being in power for three weeks and China was back in the hands of warlords. From the South, Sun Yat-sen tried to fight them and to arouse national interest but was unsuccessful.

In 1919, after the First World War, at the Versailles Peace Conference, it was decided that the German concessions in Shandong be handed over to Japan instead of back to the Chinese. This sparked off the "May Fourth Movement." Workers and intellectuals boycotted Japanese goods and demonstrated against foreign intervention and all things connected with feudal China. What started out as a protest at Beijing University spread to every part of the country, and became a national movement toward modernization. In the meantime, nationalists and communists fought for power.

NATIONALISTS AND COMMUNISTS When Sun Yat-sen died in 1925, Chiang Kai-shek, his colleague, took over. Chiang Kai-shek succeeded in unifying China by defeating the warlords in the North. He made Nanjing his capital. After this, he began to fight the communists who had formed a party in 1921.

The communists were driven to the southern mountains and were constantly persecuted. Unable to hold out any longer, they began a heroic journey known as the Long March. Led by Mao Zedong, they covered a distance of 7,000 miles on foot over some of the harshest parts of the country. They arrived in Shaanxi, northwest China, where they set up their headquarters.

Chiang Kai-shek was so obsessed with persecuting the communists that he ignored the danger of Japanese troops which moved into China in the 1930s. The Sino-Japanese War began in 1937 but Chiang still went on fighting the communists. One of his own generals arrested him and forced him to join forces with the communists in fighting against the Japanese, who were already occupying the eastern part of China.

Then the Second World War broke out in 1942. Defeated by the Americans in the Pacific, the Japanese moved out of China in 1945.

Civil war broke out between the Kuomintang and the communists when Chiang went back to fighting his old battle. The Kuomintang gradually weakened and in 1950 fled to Taiwan where they now rule the island as the Republic of China.

THE PEOPLE'S REPUBLIC OF CHINA

On October 1, 1949, from a rostrum overlooking Tiananmen Square, Mao Zedong declared the founding of the People's Republic of China. China was in trouble economically after so many years of fighting wars. Food production was low, industry was minimal, mortality was high and education and medicine were almost non-existent. The Communist Party of China not only had to establish a new political system, but also revive the economy and put it on par with other countries of the world.

By 1953, the economy had recovered considerably. Soon, industries were government-owned and peasants formed cooperatives. Encouraged by this success, Mao Zedong launched a campaign in 1959 known as the Great Leap Forward.

A painting depicting the declaration of the founding of the People's Republic of China by Mao Zedong on October 1, 1949.

THE GREAT LEAP FORWARD The countryside was divided into communes with about 5,000 households each. Their aim was the effective use of labor. Everyone ate in a communal hall, children were looked after in boarding schools and people worked in fields and factories doing all kinds of jobs.

During the slower months, some peasants were taken out of the communes to be put to work in small industrial plants such as steel mills. Crops began to give a higher yield, and steel production was up by as much as 50%.

Spurred on by this success, the government took more peasants out of the fields to work in factories. Agriculture began to suffer and peasants were exhausted. Then floods and droughts drove the country into famine. The campaign was aborted in 1960 but the effects of it lasted a long time.

THE CULTURAL REVOLUTION After the failure of the Great Leap Forward, some party members, including Deng Xiaoping, began to get the economy into shape again, while Mao was forced to take a back seat.

In 1966, Mao tried to regain control by starting what was to be the most damaging campaign of all— the Cultural Revolution. Claiming that China was turning into a capitalist country, Mao called on the Chinese to rebel against the "Four Olds"—old ideas, old culture, old habits and old customs. China was caught up in a frenzy of destruction. Books were burned, relics destroyed and temples torn down. Homes of intellectuals and people suspected of hanging on to the Four Olds were invaded and smashed. They and their families were either thrown into prison or sent to the countryside to work. One of them was Deng Xiaoping.

The Revolution soon got out of hand. China not only had to recover from another calamity but restore the faith of the rest of the world. This job rested with the respected Prime Minister Zhou Enlai.

Zhou Enlai died in 1976 and Mao Zedong died later that same year. With the death of Mao, the Cultural Revolution came to an end. In the power struggle that followed, Deng Xiaoping made a strong comeback.

China under Deng Xiaoping underwent reformation. The country was opened to foreigners for travel. Economic reforms helped the economy to recover. In June 1989, clashes between students demonstrating for democracy and the People's Liberation Army resulted in great loss of lives. China's international reputation has not recovered from the incident.

A demonstration in support of the Cultural Revolution. The Revolution gave rise to a group of young people called the Red Guards, who went on a rampage of destruction and humiliation. Later, troops had to be used to stop them.

GOVERNMENT

CHINA'S POLITICS IS a mixture of the ideas of Marx and Lenin combined with Mao Thought. Led by the Communist Party of China, it is a socialist state which is governed by the working class. The people of China exercise their right of rule through various people's congresses at different levels. Found in every town and district, they represent their community at decision-making meetings. Members of the congresses are elected by the people and come from different grassroots organizations, minority groups and religious groups.

The highest level of people's congresses is the National People's Congress. Thousands of representatives or deputies, as they are known, meet every year in the Great Hall of the People in Beijing to vote by secret ballot on issues affecting the country.

The National Emblem of the People's Republic of China.

Opposite: **The entrance to a government office complex in Nanjing. The lintel is inscribed with the writing of Sun Yat-sen. The words mean "all efforts are for the common good."**

TABLE OF HIERARCHY

Chinese Communist Party — — — — National People's Congress — — — — — — — — — President/ Vice President — — — — — — — China People's Political Consultative Conference
National Congress

Central Military Commission | State Council | Supreme People's Court | Supreme People's Procuratorate

Corporations | State Commissions | Ministries | Administrations, Bureaus and Offices

Soldiers in the Forbidden City. The Chinese army, known as the People's Liberation Army, comes under the Central Military Commission.

HIERARCHY

THE PRESIDENT AND VICE PRESIDENT The president is the official head of state of the People's Republic of China. The vice president sits in his place when he is unable to attend formal functions or perform formal duties.

THE NATIONAL PEOPLE'S CONGRESS The National People's Congress is the highest organization of state power in China. It has the power to amend the constitution and make laws. It also elects the president, vice president, chairman of the Central Military Commission, president of the Supreme People's Court and procurator-general. The NPC approves the nomination of the premier (prime minister) by the president and the members of the State Council. The NPC is made up of deputies elected from the provinces, autonomous regions and municipalities. Members of the NPC are elected every five years. They meet once a year in Beijing to decide on major issues of the state.

THE STATE COUNCIL The State Council is the highest authority in state administration. It enforces the laws and decisions of the NPC and has the power to adopt administrative measures and issue orders. It is made up of the premier, vice premiers, state councilors, ministers, the auditor-general and the secretary-general. The premier has overall responsibility and directs the work of the State Council.

THE CENTRAL MILITARY COMMISSION Headed by a chairman, the Central Military Commission is made up of the People's Liberation Army (PLA), the People's Armed Police Force and the Militia.

THE SUPREME PEOPLE'S COURT AND PEOPLE'S PROCURATORATE The function of the people's courts and procuratorates is to try criminal and civil cases and to maintain China's democratic socialist system.

MINISTRIES AND STATE COMMISSIONS Ministries and state commissions are part of the State Council. They are responsible for issuing orders and regulations in accordance with the law and decisions of the State Council. Some administrations and bureaus with special areas of work report directly to the State Council instead of their ministries, for example, the Economic Legislation Research Center, Nuclear Power Administration, Foreign Exports Bureau and State Administration for Taxation.

CORPORATIONS AND SPECIAL AGENCIES Some corporations report directly to the State Council while most corporations and industrial enterprises report to respective ministries and local governments. Two special agencies that report directly to the State Council are the Bank of China and the CAAC (the national airline).

In 1982, China adopted its fifth constitution since 1949. Earlier constitutions were adopted in 1949, 1954, 1975 and 1978. During the Cultural Revolution, many provisions of the constitution were not adhered to. In 1975, a new constitution was adopted because of changing conditions. The 1978 constitution renewed the power of the NPC while the 1982 constitution speeded up the reformation program known as the Four Modernizations.

Homeward bound on a donkey cart. At the lowest level, the administrative unit is the residents' committee.

ADMINISTRATIVE DIVISIONS

Under the Central Government, China is divided into 23 provinces, five autonomous regions and three municipalities. Each of these is divided into cities, counties and towns. Administrative units at the lowest level are residents' committees which report to the relevant provincial governments. They manage public welfare, settle disputes, see to public security and ensure that state rules are observed and implemented. It is also within their authority to adopt, issue and decide on plans for the economic and social welfare of their districts.

China's five autonomous regions are Inner Mongolia, Ningxia, Xinjiang, Guangxi and Tibet (Xizang). These areas have large communities of minority nationalities living there. Local people's congresses and governments are set up to exercise the right of self-government within the limits set by the Central Government.

The three municipalities, Beijing, Shanghai and Tianjin, report directly to the Central Government.

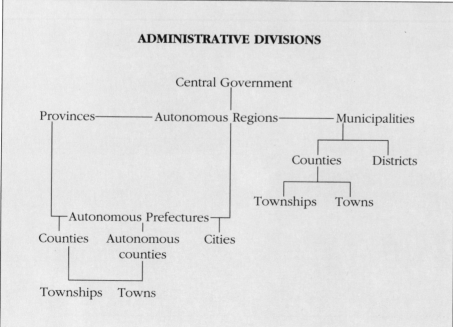

ADMINISTRATIVE DIVISIONS

Central Government

Provinces———————Autonomous Regions—————Municipalities

Counties   Districts

Townships   Towns

Autonomous Prefectures

Counties   Autonomous   Cities
counties

Townships   Towns

The Great Hall of the People, on Tiananmen Square, Beijing, was built in 1959 and completed in less than a year. It is here that the National People's Congress meets, and formal meetings and receptions for visiting heads of state and government take place.

ECONOMY

AFTER THE LIBERATION of 1949, all enterprises were confiscated and turned over to the Communist government. Production from agriculture, handicrafts, industries and commerce came under public ownership. This system of public ownership meant that everyone contributed to and benefited from a common goal.

In the 1980s, China embarked on economic reforms aimed at making it a powerful socialist economy by the year 2000. China opened its doors to foreign trade and foreign investments. Special economic zones were set up where foreign investors were attracted to build factories and operate businesses.

To encourage workers to work hard, a bonus system was introduced. Besides their low basic wage, workers got bonuses for being productive, punctual, for perfect attendance and for having a good work attitude.

With the new economic policy, Chinese for the first time in many years could own small businesses. Farmers go to the "free markets" to sell their farm produce. At these open-air makeshift markets, other small businesses sell cooked food, clothes, toys, books, and every imaginable product. New services such as tailoring, hairdressing and entertainment cater to the needs of a more affluent China.

Above: **A free market in Lijiang, where farmers take their excess produce to sell, after meeting the government quota.**

Opposite: **A streetside basket weaver. During the slower months on the farms, farmers take on part-time work such as street vending or basket weaving.**

37

Rice terraces in south-western China. China grows enough rice for its own use and for export.

AGRICULTURE

China is mainly an agricultural country. About 10% of the vast expanse of China is suitable for cultivation. This means that about 300,000,000 acres of land are used to grow food to feed 1 billion, making China the largest producer of food in the world.

In the North where the weather is cold, harsh and dry, wheat is grown and made into bread and noodles. Other grains that are grown in the North are millet and sorghum. Sorghum is used as a food substitute and fodder and sometimes made into wine. Millet and sorghum are quick and easy to grow and are often grown alongside wheat. In case a drought kills the wheat, there would still be a harvest of millet and sorghum.

Very little rice is grown in the North, but it is the most important crop in the South. Rice is grown on half of the cultivated land in China and crops are harvested twice a year.

THE BACKBONE OF THE ECONOMY

The peasants of China make up 80% of the population and are the backbone of the economy. They alone make up one-third of all the farmers in the world. After Liberation, the structure of the countryside was reorganized. Co-operatives, and later communes, were formed in which peasants pooled their land and resources together and shared whatever income they got.

In 1979, a system was started whereby a peasant household was

allowed to work on a piece of land and, in return, had to deliver to the government an agreed amount of produce. Peasants were allowed to keep whatever extra they produced. This yielded good results and by the mid-80s peasant families were growing products or raising animals for their own profit aside from the contracted amount.

Chinese farmers use simple tools to get their work done. Few can afford tractors or combined harvesters. In the past they even had to gather human and animal manure as fertilizers. This is seldom done nowadays as chemical fertilizers are cheap and abundant.

During the non-farming months, farmers find temporary employment in cottage industries or turn to trade, like selling cooked food or bamboo ware.

Corn and soybeans are grown both in North and South China. Soybeans, especially, are an important part of the Chinese diet. Protein-rich soybeans are made into soybean milk and other products. In the North where vegetables are scarce, soybeans are grown into bean sprouts. Soybean oil is used to make soap and paint, and exported as a raw material.

On the flat grasslands of Mongolia, animals such as sheep and goats are raised. Mutton makes up a large part of the northern diet. China now produces enough mutton for its own consumption and for export as well. Dairy products come from cows raised on the outskirts of large cities.

Non-food crops include cotton, rapeseed, tobacco and silk.

A metalworks plant in Wuhan. Steel and iron smelting are top money-earning industries.

Opposite: The port at Shanghai is one of the main ports in China, handling the largest amount of freight in China annually.

CHINA'S REVENUE

China has a fairly comprehensive industrial system. It does not depend heavily on imported finished products as the country manufactures its own electrical appliances and other consumer goods. It also produces its own cars, trucks, planes, trains, ships and heavy industrial equipment.

China is rich in raw materials. It has large amounts of coal and minerals such as tungsten, antimony, tin, bauxite, manganese, lead, zinc and copper, which it exports.

Top money-earning industries are oil, steel and iron, coal, electrical energy, machine building, textiles and light industries.

In 1990 alone, more than $1 billion worth of goods each were exported to Hong Kong, Germany, the Soviet Union and Singapore. These ranged from agricultural products like meat and grain to raw materials like coal, crude and refined oil, cement and rolled steel. China, in turn, imported $1 billion worth of goods each from Hong Kong and Macau, Japan, the United States, West Germany, the Soviet Union, Taiwan, Canada and Britain.

China's industrial cities used to be scattered along the coast, but efforts have been made to develop industrial areas and towns throughout the country.

SPECIAL ECONOMIC ZONES

In 1979, Shenzhen, a little town in Guangdong, was developed into an economic zone which manufactured and processed products from the country. It served as a showcase for foreign investors with capital and technology. At the same time, China established three other economic zones in Zhuhai, Shantou (both also in Guangdong province) and Xiamen (in Fujian province).

These economic zones were set up because China realized that in order to catch up with the rest of the world, they not only needed foreign money, but also foreign technology and expertise. To attract foreign investors, China needed to have more flexible economic policies. The solution was to set up economic zones to which foreign businesses were attracted by favorable terms such as in the use of land and in income tax payment.

Shenzhen, the first economic zone to be developed, is just next to Hong Kong. Investors are attracted by Shenzhen's reduced taxes, low wages and operating costs and cheap, abundant labor. Shenzhen also has land and raw materials and its proximity to Hong Kong brings it closer to world markets.

In 1988, the tropical island of Hainan became China's latest and largest economic zone.

CHINESE

TWENTY PERCENT or 1.2 billion of the world's population live in China. Most of the Chinese live along the fertile coastal areas of the Yang Zi river delta. The most populous province is Sichuan with 107 million people (487 per square mile) and the least populous is Tibet with 2.2 million people (4.7 per square mile). Although cities are crowded, over 80% of the population live in the countryside—China has the greatest number of farmers in the world.

HAN CHINESE

China's main ethnic group is the Han Chinese who originated around the Yellow, Yang Zi and Pearl rivers. They make up over 1 billion people and are the largest ethnic group in China and the world.

MINORITIES

Apart from the Hans which comprise 95% of China's population, there are 55 other ethnic groups. Most of them are scattered along the border regions of India, Afghanistan, the Soviet Union and Vietnam. The biggest minority group is the Zhuangs with 13.5 million people, while the smallest is that of the Hezhe with little more than 1,000 people. Although small in number, minorities occupy 50% to 60% of China's total land area, living mainly in autonomous regions.

Minorities have their own languages. Putonghua is taught in schools, but they are encouraged to pass on their language and customs to their children.

An outing (*opposite*) and returning home from the market (*below*). Han Chinese make up 95% of China's population.

There are more than 4 million Manchus, half of whom live in northeast China. They have their own script and language. China's rulers from 1644 to 1911, they have added to the richness of the Chinese culture, including books written in Han Chinese.

Most of the 1.7 million Koreans live in northeast China, the rest in major Chinese cities. They have their own spoken and written language and have their own newspapers. Koreans are fond of music and love to sing and dance at festivities.

Huis, at 7.2 million, are one of China's largest minorities. They are Moslems who live mainly in the northwest, although they are also scattered throughout China. One outstanding Hui is the famous Ming dynasty voyager Zheng He.

Kazakhs number nearly 1 million and live mainly in Xinjiang in the northwest. They have a written language. Many Kazakhs live by animal husbandry and move from place to place looking for pasture, living in tents called *yurt*.

The 2,100 Llobas live mainly in southeastern Tibet. Largely farmers, Llobas are also skilled at crafts. Hunting is important to them and young boys start early, joining adults in hunting trips. Staple foods include corn or millet dumplings.

The more than 5 million Yis live in southwest China, in mountain areas, mainly as farmers. They have their own written language, with a colorful literature. Yi women live in their own parents' home after marriage, until their first child is born.

 Dais live in southern Yunnan province in southwest China. The staple food for the Dais is rice, eaten with sour and hot dishes of fish, meats and vegetables. Dais live in two-level houses built on stilts. Many of the Dais are Buddhists.

 At more than 5 million, the Miaos are one of the largest minorities living in southwest China. Miaos love to sing and their songs may be as long as 15,000 lines. They are also skilled craftsmen, although farming is a main occupation.

 With more than 13 million people, Zhuangs are China's largest minority group. Most of them live in Guangxi in southwest China. They are reputed for their singing. Young people choose their lovers at song festivals through songs.

 The 12,000 Jings live in southwest China mainly as farmers, their main crops being rice, sweet potato, peanut and millet. They read and write the Han script and speak Cantonese, having lived among the Hans for a long time.

 The 800,000 Lis live on Hainan, the second largest island in China. The tropical island to the south of the mainland is fertile and the Lis reap as many as three crops of rice a year. The Lis are known for their knowledge of herbal medicine.

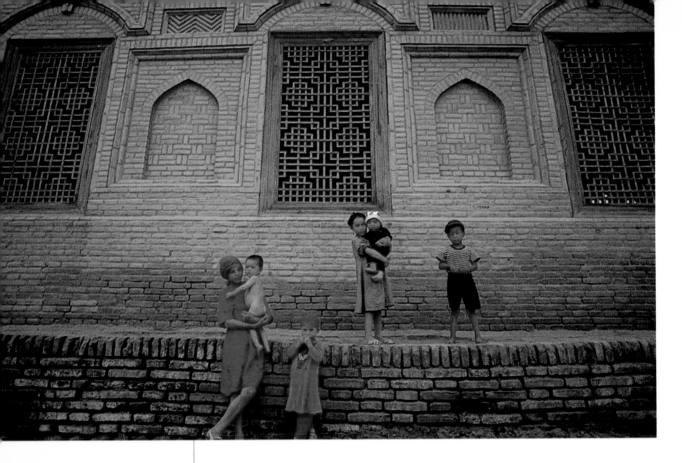

Above: **Uygur children outside a mosque.**

Below and bottom: **A Tibetan and an Uygur couple in traditional dress.**

TIBETANS Tibet sits on a plateau that is 14,000 feet above sea level. Surrounded on three sides by the highest mountains in the world, its remoteness and inaccessibility adds to its mystery and fascination. Tibetans are a religious people and their life revolves around Lamaism, a form of Buddhism. Tibetans believe in reincarnation and the Dalai Lama, exiled by the Chinese government, is revered as a reincarnating Buddha-to-be.

Tibetans are a friendly and hospitable people who are wonderful singers and dancers. Their main occupation is farming and raising cattle. Their diet consists mainly of the grains they grow. Their favorite drink is *tsampa*, which is hot tea with ground barley and yak butter.

UYGURS Most of the Uygurs live in Xinjiang province in northwestern China. They have settled in and around the oases of the Taklamakan Desert, cultivating fruit and grain and raising sheep and horses. The Uygurs, who are Moslems, speak a language similar to Turkish and their written language is Arabic.

MONGOLIANS Mongolians are a nomadic people who live on the northern grasslands of the Mongolian plains. For most months of the year, Mongolians move from place to place in search of new pastures for their cattle. Because of this, they live in portable homes called *yurt*.

These are tents made of animal hide supported by strong wooden poles. The cylindrical walls are padded with thick felt to keep out the cold in the winter months. On the roof, skylights also act as air vents for warming fires.

In summer, the base of the walls can be lifted up to let the cool breeze in. It is during this time that Mongolians, whose main livelihood is raising cattle and horses, move around in search of grazing pastures. It is no wonder that their main diet consists of dairy products, meat and grain. Vegetables, especially the leafy variety, are a rarity, so what they eat most are bean sprouts, which can be grown anywhere in any season. Meat is often air-dried and it is often common to see strips of mutton hanging inside and outside a *yurt*. Mongolians love tea boiled with milk from their cattle. Sometimes, butter-fried millet is added to it to improve the taste.

Mongolians are skilled horsemen and archers. They also enjoy wrestling, singing and dancing. Television has entered the lives of these nomads and evenings often find them in front of a television run by a generator outside their *yurt*.

Top: **Mongolian women in their tent.**

Above: **Mongolians in traditional dress.**

47

THE OVERSEAS CHINESE

Poverty, wars and rebellions forced many Chinese to leave their country in search of a better life. Most left from provinces in South China such as Guangdong, Fujian and Shanghai. Some left for countries in nearby Southeast Asia such as Thailand, Malaysia, Singapore and Indonesia while others as far away as Europe, Africa, the Caribbean, South America, Australia, Canada and the United States where many settled in "The Golden Mountain" (California) to dig for gold or to build railways.

Overseas Chinese, or Hua Qiao, practice their own customs and traditions. Some of these are not practiced by the mainland Chinese today as China is now a socialist country that does not allow free practice of such customs.

The Hua Qiao community is a large one. There are about 32 million Chinese living outside China. Many of those who left their provinces and made a better living than back home often sent for their male relatives. This is why we find large groups from a particular province in one country. California, for example, has a large Cantonese community and Brazil has many from Fujian province.

The wish of some Hua Qiao is to go back to their home town. Many who have made good have returned to rebuild their ancestral home or make donations to build schools, hospitals and public buildings in their villages or provinces.

POPULATION CONTROL

China has always been a populous country. This is because it is an agricultural country and more children means less work for all. Another reason is that Chinese believe that the more sons one has, the better one will be looked after in old age. Also, the family name will be passed down to future generations.

With arable land so scarce in China, this poses a great food problem. On top of this, the population grows at an annual rate of 17 million, meaning there are more mouths to feed each year. Another problem is housing, particularly in the cities where two or three generations live in a one-bedroom apartment.

A poster exhorting the people to plan their family.

In 1982, family planning was made a state policy. Late marriage and having fewer, healthier babies at a later age was encouraged. City dwellers are limited to only one child per couple, there being penalties for having more. Lucky couples with twins or triplets are admired and envied as their children will not be penalized. Couples in the countryside can get permission to have another child if their first one is a daughter. Family planning also extends to the minority areas but is not strictly enforced.

Family planning education starts young. "Puberty education" makes teenagers aware of their physical changes, and correct attitudes toward sex and marriage are taught. When they grow up, they are given lectures in family planning before and after marriage.

In rural areas, where prejudices and customs still persist, the State Family Planning Commissioner gives lectures on contraceptives and family planning to farmers.

LIBRARY
LYNDHURST HIGH SCHOOL
LYNDHURST, N. J.

LIFESTYLE

THE CHINESE ATTITUDE toward life is influenced by Confucian ethics, which teach Chinese to respect and love their fellowmen.

PERSON TO PERSON

Chinese will go through all means not to embarrass another person, whether friend or foe. They never say "no" to any request or outwardly disagree with anything. They have been brought up to mask their feelings, often by smiling or laughing. If someone responds to a request with "later" and later "forgets," it probably means that he or she cannot do the favor.

When two Chinese get to know each other, they have established *guanxi*, or relations. They are obliged to do each other favors; one never says no to the other person, but "later" or "maybe."

Chinese are also super hosts. Tables are often filled with food even after dinner is through. This seems like an incredible waste, but to the Chinese, empty plates mean their guests are still hungry and they have failed as hosts.

Chinese modesty does not allow them to receive flattery, but to give it. Compliments are often brushed aside with an embarrassed laugh and a returned compliment.

Mother and child (*opposite*) and a little chat and bird song to pass the day with (*below*). To the Chinese, the community in which they live is very important—it provides them with social support, be it job-hunting, a death in the family or just socializing.

Children address older people who are not relatives as "*ah yi*" (aunt) or "*shushu*" (uncle). This indicates that they respect these adults as much as their own aunts or uncles.

FORMS OF ADDRESS

Chinese have a title for every member of the household. This came about because historically the Chinese family was an extended one with several generations living under one roof, and one had to be able to identify everyone's position in the family.

Chinese never ask how many brothers and sisters one has, but how many are older or younger than one. Elder brothers are called "*gege*" while younger ones are "*didi.*" "*Jiejie*" refers to elder sisters while younger ones are called "*meimei.*" Different sets of names are given to each maternal and paternal grandparent and each aunt and uncle. Imagine the confusion with distant cousins and their in-laws.

Outside the family, Chinese of all ages are known by their surname. Most of the time, "*xiao,*" meaning "little," is used as a prefix for younger people and "*lao,*" meaning "old," is put in front of the surname of a

THE CHINESE NAME

The Chinese name consists of three words. The surname comes first, then the generation name and last, the given name. The surname is the proudest thing a Chinese inherits. It is by this name that he or she is known outside the family.

The generation name denotes the generation in which a person is born. Often, brothers and male cousins share one name. There are no generation names for girls as the Chinese feel that when girls marry, they belong to another family. In rural villages where often the whole town shares the same surname, there will be a book of generation names. It is possible to trace which generation a great-great-great grandfather belonged to just by referring to it.

Families now do away with the generation name as parents often have one child. Most children today have names consisting only of the surname and the given name.

Careful thought goes into the choice of a name. Parents often choose names that reflect virtues or talents they hope their children will possess. Feminine names such as "Li" meaning "beauty" or "Fang" meaning "fragrant" are common. Boys possess masculine names such as "Qiang" meaning "strength" and "Wei" meaning "greatness." (Picture shows a page from a book of family names.)

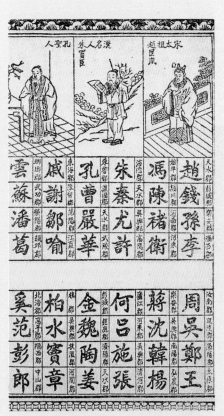

middle-aged person to show respect for his or her age and experience. These prefixes are used only for persons one is familiar with. In formal address, the surname is put before "*xiansheng*" (mister). Women keep their maiden names after marriage, replacing "miss" with "madam" behind their surnames.

Teachers are well respected and "*laoshi*," meaning "teacher," is always added behind their surnames. Often, people in the streets address strangers as "*tongzhi*," or "comrade," when asking for directions or buying things.

A grandmother with her grandchildren. Older folk are looked after by their children in their old age.

THE EXTENDED FAMILY

In China, life revolves around the family. It is often common to find three generations living together under one roof in the city, while in the countryside it can extend to include uncles, aunts, numerous cousins and in-laws.

The oldest relative in the family is always looked upon as a person of wisdom whose word is usually law. Old folks are well looked after even if they are ill or bedridden. They are only sent to hospitals or institutions if the family cannot provide them with the proper care.

The greatest joy for the older generation is to see the whole family around them—the more males the better, as they are assured that the family name will be carried on.

The family hierarchy is carefully preserved and each member of the family knows where he or she stands even if the difference in age is only a few days. The younger generation is not expected to talk back or disobey orders.

Babies are well-loved in any Chinese family. With the one-child policy implemented across China, the precious child is doted on and given almost everything it asks for. In the extended family, baby is certainly king.

Adult Chinese live with their families until the time they marry. Upon marriage, the woman moves into the man's parents' home. The main reason why a Chinese man lives at his parents' home is that it is a child's duty to look after his parents until their death.

GOING TO SCHOOL

Children in China start school at the age of six and a half. Urban children go to school for six full days a week, have only six weeks off during

summer and four weeks in winter, and four examinations a year.

The school day starts at eight in the morning, with four periods of 50 minutes each. There is a 10-minute break between periods and a two-hour break for lunch. Afternoons are devoted to more lessons, self-study, extracurricular activities or doing chores around the school. The school day ends at about five or six in the evening.

Elementary school lasts for six years, after which children go to high school. High school is divided into three years of junior high and three years of senior high education. Students can choose to do vocational training after junior high school. This prepares them for specialized jobs. Students who finish senior high school can take entrance examinations to universities or institutes that specialize in languages, research, teaching or physical training.

Children in the countryside spend less time in the classroom. They take time off during the planting and harvesting seasons to help out on the land. They go to schools nearest to their farms, where they learn basic education. Sometimes this could mean a two- or three-hour walk starting at dawn to make it to school at eight.

Playtime in school. Some of the subjects taught in high school are mathematics, a foreign language, politics, history, geography, sciences, music and art. In the countryside, agricultural high schools can be found, where students are taught agricultural science and technology.

Workers of a small paper mill. All workers in China, and their families, are looked after by their work unit.

THE ROLE OF THE WORK UNIT

The work unit, or *danwei*, plays an important role in the life of the Chinese. They and their family are looked after by this organization from the time they start work until the time they die. An entire corporation or several small factories could make one *danwei*.

The *danwei* looks after a family's medical fees and subsidizes living expenses, heating costs, newspaper subscriptions and even transportation and bicycle-repair expenses. A little money is given to working mothers toward child welfare and bonuses are given for long service. These are basic benefits given by all work units though some might vary.

Some *danwei* own blocks of flats or rows of houses so that colleagues live near each other and near their place of work. These houses are heavily subsidized and rent can be as cheap as $10 a month including utilities.

A *danwei* is an integral part of Chinese life. No major decisions are made without first consulting it. A couple intending to marry must get the

WOMEN IN CHINA

The women of ancient China were always homebound, controlled people. Girls had their feet bound when they were between four and eight years old to stop their feet from growing. This painful process left them with misshapened, club-like feet when they grew older. With their tiny feet supporting their weight, they could only manage small steps at a time and, with a gait like "a swaying willow tree," were deemed attractive creatures. It also kept them from venturing too far from the home. Fortunately, this habit died off in the 20th century.

After China became a republic, the status of Chinese women was raised to that of being equal to men. Women played a big part in rebuilding China. Most took on jobs once only held by men such as doctors, engineers, factory workers, soldiers and even jobs involving manual labor, such as farmers and porters.

Children are well taken care of from an early age by nurseries while their mothers join the workforce. Women are paid equally with men and carry the same workload as their male counterparts. Men share responsibilities for their children, do household chores like cleaning and ironing and many instead of yelling "What's for dinner?" cook it.

Women are well represented in the government, in the various congresses, and hold key positions in large organizations. It is felt that if any one can do a job, they should be given the responsibility regardless of sex.

approval of the *danwei* first. Likewise, if they are thinking of a divorce, the *danwei* will see if they can settle their differences without splitting up.

Permission from a *danwei* is also needed if a Chinese intends to go out of the country. Chinese are only allowed to travel on official business or on a scholarship. They can only vacation within the country.

A Chinese worker cannot be fired, and for those who intend to switch jobs, their new *danwei* must apply to have them released. Only when their present *danwei* signs the release papers can they take a new position.

MARRIAGE

In the days of old, marriage used to be an elaborate affair with days of feasting and complicated rites. The wedding day would be the first time the bride and groom actually set eyes on each other as marriages were pre-arranged by parents.

Nowadays, couples choose whom they want to marry but must seek the approval of their *danwei*. If approval is given, they can register their marriage. This is a simple civil ceremony, after which they may arrange a celebration. Usually, an auspicious date will be picked. A popular date is the seventh day of the seventh moon. It is said that this is the only day that a fairy from heaven gets to meet her mortal husband.

Autumn months are popular for weddings, when the weather is good and the moon is at its brightest. Many also get married during the winter months as work on the farm is relatively slow and time can be spent cooking a feast for the whole village.

Marriage preparations include the groom's family buying electrical appliances such as a refrigerator for the couple's new home. There is also a trousseau and jewelry for the bride. On the wedding day, the groom makes his way to the bride's house in a bus hired for the occasion. The bride and groom are dressed in new, everyday suits, though the white wedding gown is becoming popular. They then go to the groom's house where the bride will meet the new family and from there on the celebrations begin.

Below: **Wedding couples in the city usually hold a dinner for family and friends. But it is increasingly popular for them to put their money toward a honeymoon or new home. If so, they announce their wedding by treating family and friends to some candy.**

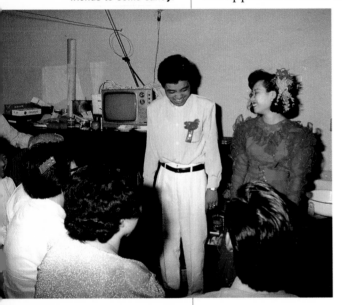

Opposite: **Mother and child are confined to the home as far as possible during the first month after birth. On the day the child is one month old, a celebration is held, after which the mother is said to be fit enough for normal work.**

CHILDBIRTH

There is often great excitement when a baby is expected. The mother is well looked after and well fed. Chinese mothers usually hold full-time jobs and carry on whatever they are doing until the seventh month of pregnancy when they are given lighter tasks. In the city, mothers are given anything from 56 days up to a year of paid maternity leave.

Customs concerning childbirth are more prevalent in the countryside than in the city. Pregnant women are not allowed to join in any social occasions, especially weddings and funerals, from the start of their pregnancy to 100 days after the child is delivered.

There are more taboos after birth, perhaps because some homes are far from medical facilities and prevention is better than cure. Women are not allowed to bathe, wash their hair or do any household chores for one month after the birth of their child.

During this time, they are brought back to strength with plenty of rest and good food. Fresh, uncooked fruit and vegetables are avoided as they are believed to be too *yin,* or cooling, to the system and may cause the mother to fall ill. The new mother's diet consists mainly of noodles, eggs and chicken. Fresh anchovies are often made into a soup in the belief that drinking it increases the milk supply.

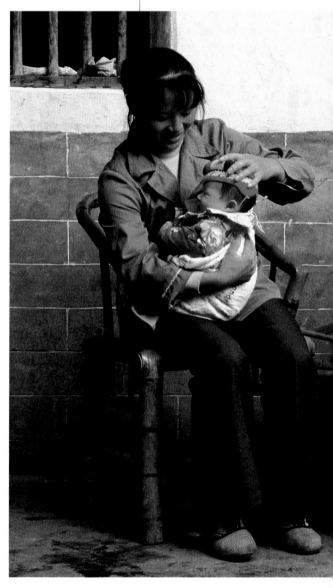

Paper objects representing houses, money, clothes and others are burned at the funeral, so that the deceased is well provided for in the "Yellow Spring," or the Chinese Hades.

DEATH

When a person dies, his or her *danwei* is informed and officials are sent to see if they can help in any way with the funeral arrangements and pay for certain funeral expenses.

The body is taken to the nearest crematorium, bathed and dressed in funeral clothes. It is then placed in a glass coffin for friends and family to pay their last respects before cremation. After cremation, the ashes are placed in a special box and put in the crematorium or taken home.

In the countryside, where burial is more common than cremation, people make their own elaborately decorated coffins. Preparations for death start when a person is still alive. Once people reach 50 years or so, they or their children will start making a coffin. Once it is done, it is stored in the house until the time comes. It sounds morbid, but these older people are happy to know that their children will carry out the last rites.

Death rites in the countryside start with a wake that can last up to one week. Friends and relatives come from near and far to partake in a feast and pay their last respects. The family of the deceased are dressed in white hoods and robes. Sacrificial items like paper money, paper houses and paper cars are burned to make sure the deceased is comfortable in the other life. The coffin is then buried on a plot of family land.

The government is trying to discourage the practice of burials as this means that precious agricultural land will be taken up by tombs.

THE CHINESE HOME

Whether down in the country or in a busy urban city, Chinese homes are small and simply furnished. Chinese take pride in neatness and houses are seldom found in a mess.

In the countryside, houses are more spacious. They are often walled up, with a simple wooden door opening into a courtyard. On either side of the courtyard are a kitchen and a storeroom or extra bedroom. Facing the entrance is the main hall, consisting of the living room and one or two bedrooms. There is often a water pipe in the kitchen and in the courtyard. Toilet facilities are found outside the house and shared by two or three families.

An apartment block in Guangxi. Chinese homes are often dimly lit. In cities, there is often a day in a week without electricity. Authorities believe these cuts save more than the inconvenience they cause.

These houses are also found in the cities. They are very cramped as sometimes three or four families share a common courtyard. More fortunate city dwellers live in hard-to-attain apartments. These may contain a kitchen, hall, bedroom and toilet. Homes seldom have bathrooms and, often, the only source of water supply is the kitchen sink. Most companies provide shower facilities on their premises for their staff. There are also public baths. The living room is often a multi-function room used to entertain guests, have meals and, at night, serve as an extra bedroom. Every available space is used for storage. It is common to see boxes of belongings stacked on cupboards, under beds and along corridors. Even window sills are put to good use, storing or drying food for the winter.

THE CHINESE COSTUME

Above: **Beijing street, a sea of blue and green, with men and women, soldiers and civilians, dressed in the Mao suit.**

Opposite: **Chinese herbs include dried lotus leaves, lotus seeds, ginseng roots and boxthorn berries.**

Most Chinese wear Western-styled clothes. Chinese adults own at least one Mao suit. Usually made of thick, dark blue cotton, it is a simple tunic with buttons down the front.

The Mao suit made its appearance around the time China became a republic. It was first used as a uniform in the army and later became widely used even by civilians. Its simple design and tough fabric saw many people through lean times when all they needed was something warm and lasting.

Women also took to wearing Mao suits. Before the Cultural Revolution, women wore long, slim dresses with modest slits up the side to formal functions. They were later discouraged but have since made a comeback.

THE RED SCARF

These are worn like a brownie scarf by elementary school children. This red scarf represents a corner of the Chinese flag and is worn by members of the Young Pioneers League. This club is a like a junior section of the Communist Party. The scarf is formally handed over at a ceremony when children are 14 years old. They later choose whether or not they want to join the Communist Party's Youth League.

TRADITIONAL CHINESE MEDICINE

Traditional Chinese medicine is taken not just to relieve a symptom or cure an illness but also to improve body functions. Brews of herbs, leaves, bark and berries are cooked for hours before being drunk in bowls. Sometimes more exotic items such as animal horns, dried snakes, lizards and fat glands from the Manchurian snow frog are added for a more potent brew.

Traditional Chinese medicine has its origins in the countryside where people discovered by trial and error that combinations of certain herbs relieved certain ailments. Books listing herbs and their functions were written as far back as the Han dynasty.

A Chinese pharmacy consists of a large hall with counters on all sides. Behind the counters are drawers which cover the walls. Each drawer holds a certain herb and prescriptions are made up by combining several kinds of herbs. There is usually a doctor of Chinese medicine in attendance. By taking the patient's pulse, looking at the color of the tongue and skin, and noting the symptoms, the doctor can diagnose the problem. A simple headache can be linked to organs like the liver or kidneys that are temporarily under stress and not functioning well. Medicine is prescribed to relieve the headache and a tonic recommended to get the organ back to normal. As herbs are slow-acting, they have to be taken over a long period of time.

Chinese look after their health well. Often, mothers make tonic soups for the whole family. Besides herbal medicine, traditional medical treatment includes massage, deep breathing exercises and acupuncture.

An acupuncture chart from the *Wei Jing*, or *Treatise on the Stomach*, from a Chinese encyclopedia of the early 17th century.

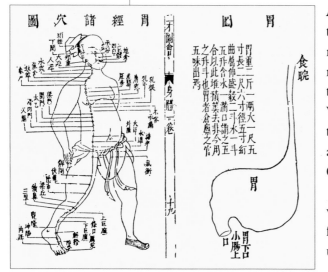

ACUPUNCTURE Acupuncture is based on the Chinese theory that the body has a network of energy lines known as meridians. These meridians are linked and they affect the major organs of the body. When a person is not feeling well, it is thought that there is an imbalance of *yin* and *yang* or an uneven distribution of *qi* (energy, or force).

Along the meridians are certain points where needles are placed to get the *qi* to flow again. Different sizes of needles are used to pierce the skin at varying angles

YIN AND YANG

It is the Taoist belief that the human body holds two intertwining forces, *yin* and *yang*. *Yin* is represented by femininity, darkness, cold and water. *Yang* is masculinity, sun, heat and fire.

This does not mean that a female possesses only *yin* qualities. A very active girl who is always perspiring and prone to fevers and sore throats will be thought to be more *yang* than *yin* and her mother will make her eat more foods with *yin* properties.

An imbalance in *yin* and *yang* within the body causes illnesses and discomfort. A Chinese will try to correct this by deciding if he or she is too *yin* or too *yang*. *Yin* symptoms could be a cough with a heavy chest, rheumatic pains or dizziness. *Yang* symptoms could be a fever, rash, or sore throat.

If the discomforts are simple, home cures in the form of food included in a meal could relieve a patient. Foods fall into three categories. Hot, cooling and neutral. For example, cucumbers, watercress and fruit are cooling, while garlic, peppers and chives are hot.

The same theory is applied at a Chinese pharmacy. Patients are treated with scrapings of rhinoceros horns to cool a fever or tiger-bone wine to cure aches and pains. Chinese medicine and diet regulate the body system and bring the body to its original equilibrium.

and depths. They are then twirled or vibrated by hand or electronically until a numbing sensation is felt. It is this sensation that the acupuncturist is aiming for to relieve the ailment.

There are over 300 acupuncture points throughout the body and it is common practice to stick needles in the ears, on the face and neck and in between the fingers and toes.

Like traditional Chinese herbal medicine, acupuncture should be carried out over a period of time to be fully effective. It is most commonly used as an anaesthetic in China and in countries abroad. This way, even major operations can be done with the patient fully conscious and feeling no pain at all.

RELIGION

TO THE MAJORITY OF CHINESE, religion is a mixture of all the various Chinese philosophies. A Chinese who is not a Christian or Moslem often integrates Taoist, Confucian and Buddhist beliefs.

Taoism, Confucianism and Buddhism began as philosophies. Their teachings relate to harmonious living between man and nature. They later became popular religions, and were mixed up by the Chinese so that, for example, a Taoist may have Confucian and Buddhist beliefs.

Chinese are generally superstitious due to the Taoist belief in keeping harmony with nature and the universe. If good luck can be brought to a major event like a marriage or moving to new premises, it will be done. This often means choosing an auspicious date and time on the lunar calendar, when the moon is full or when zodiac signs do not clash. Fire crackers are let off to scare away offending spirits and red is used almost everywhere to attract good fortune. Being over-superstitious is frowned on by the Chinese authorities as it inhibits one's thinking and actions. The younger generation is less superstitious than those born before Liberation.

Although the Constitution of 1982 guarantees religious freedom, a majority of the Chinese population remain atheist as most grew up during the Cultural Revolution, during which religious groups were persecuted.

MAIN RELIGIONS

TAOISM Taoism was founded by Lao Zi, whose name means "old master." Taoism teaches man to live in harmony with nature. Taoists believe in supernatural beings, use charms and spells, meditate and keep a vegetarian diet. It is their belief that these practices can help them gain immortality and be one with the universe.

Above: **A statue of Chinese philosopher Confucius.**

Opposite: **The Lokapala, one of many deities worshiped by Chinese.**

Taoist priests at prayer. The Taoist book, *Dao De Jing,* or *Book of the Way,* is an ancient text containing only 5,000 words. It was one of few texts spared by Qin Shihuang and was first translated into Latin by Jesuit missionaries in the 18th century.

CONFUCIANISM Born in 551 B.C., Confucius was a government official who became a teacher of moral ethics later in his life. His philosophy became the backbone of Chinese thinking and behavior.

Confucius lived at a time of political violence and social disorder. Disturbed by what was going on around him, he devoted his life to the teaching of *ren*, or the love of man. Linked to this is *xiao*, or filial piety, devotion to one's parents. This devotion continues after the death of the parents in the form of ancestral worship. Tablets bearing the name of the deceased are found in homes and the deceased are honored and remembered especially on birthdays and death anniversaries.

Some of the other qualities connected with *ren* are loyalty, courage, wisdom and trustworthiness. The aim of cultivating such qualities is to become a superior man. Thus, Confucianism also encouraged interest in the arts as they stimulate the mind.

BUDDHISM Buddhism was brought to China along the Silk Road by

Indian merchants. By the 6th century it was established as a major religion in China. Chinese monks journeyed to India and Sri Lanka to bring back Sanskrit scriptures and sutras which were translated into Chinese. Traveling monks also made important records of their journeys which have become important fiction and nonfiction literature. In most parts of China, the Buddhist philosophy absorbs Taoist and Confucian aspects while in Tibet, another sect of Buddhism is practiced. Lamaism is a blend of Buddhism and Bon, an indigenous ancient religion of Tibet.

A Tibetan Lama Buddhist monk.

ISLAM Islam also came with merchants round about the 7th century. Scholars and missionaries arrived and mosques were built. Ten minority groups such as the Uygurs, Kazakhs and Tartars make up a large part of the Moslem community. Another large community of Moslems are the Huis. They are ethnic Hans who are staunch Moslems and are the only group of people recognized as minorities because of their religion.

CHRISTIANITY The earliest Christians to arrive in China, in A.D. 735, were the Nestorian Christians from Syria. In the 13th century, the Jesuits came and brought with them scientific knowledge. When China opened up to the world after the Opium Wars, Protestant and Roman Catholic missionaries arrived. Although Christian missionaries opened schools, universities and hospitals, Christianity never became a popular religion in China.

The Kai Yuan Temple in Fujian province. Buddha images fill the main prayer hall.

THE CHINESE TEMPLE

The Chinese temple is one of the most interesting places to visit in China. Its halls are filled with statues of deities, gods and demigods. Some of these are celestial beings, others mythical characters and some elevated from the status of mere mortals because of their brave or outstanding feats during their lifetime.

A pair of door gods guard the main entrances. They are said to have guarded a passage used by spirits a long, long time ago. Wicked ones were weeded out by these door gods, bound and fed to tigers. It became a tradition to paint their images on temple doors to scare away any evil spirits that might want to slip in.

One of the most popular goddesses is Guan Yin. She is said to manifest herself in thousands of forms. Also known as the Goddess of Mercy, she is said to look kindly on her followers and rescue them from calamities and worldly problems.

WIND AND WATER

Feng shui, or wind and water, is about living in harmony with the natural environment and tapping the goodness of nature for good fortune and health. It was first practiced in ancient China by farmers, to whom wind and water were very important natural forces that could either destroy or nurture their crops.

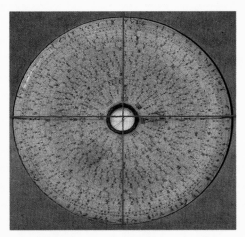

Feng shui has developed into an art of locating buildings and other man-made structures (for example, fountains and bridges) to harmonize with and benefit from the surrounding physical environment. Chinese believe that there are invisible forces beneath the earth and that the forces are positive (*yang*) and negative (*yin*). They invented a compass called a *luopan* to measure these forces. A balance of the two forces in a person's immediate surroundings is important for good health and fortune. For example, in a room, warm colors (positive force) should be balanced by cool colors (negative force) if the person living in it is to be at peace.

According to *feng shui*, best building sites have a hill protecting the back of the building, and calm water in front to provide a soothing view. A huge tree that shadows the main entrance could prevent fortune from entering, while a swift flowing drain or river nearby could be carrying all the luck away. Doors are sometimes built at an angle to prevent bad luck from entering and mirrors are hung above doors or windows to scare away evil spirits by their own reflections.

In every nook and cranny of the temple, deities, such as those of health, wealth and longevity, are found, plus various buddhas. The most popular of the buddhas is the smiling buddha, a bald, smiling character with an outstanding belly. He is a favorite as his disposition represents wealth, joy and long life.

The fragrance of joss sticks fill the air and candles and oil lamps light the dim temple interiors. Worshipers give thanks for granted wishes or pray for blessings for a better life.

LANGUAGE

CHINESE SPEAK their own dialects within their own regions. These dialects vary in provinces and even from village to village. There are eight major dialects in China.

MAJOR DIALECTS

The northern dialect or Bei Fang Hua forms the basis of China's official language, and is spoken by Chinese living in the northern, central and southwestern provinces of China. More than 70% of the Chinese population speak this dialect.

The Wu dialect is spoken by people around Shanghai, Jiangsu and Zhejiang provinces. Xiang is spoken in Hunan province, the Gan dialect spoken in Jiangxi and Hubei provinces, and Kejia (Hakka) is spoken in parts of Guangdong, Fujian and Jiangxi provinces. The northern Min dialect is spoken in parts of Fujian and Taiwan, while southern Min is spoken throughout the south of Fujian province, parts of Hainan, most of Taiwan and by many overseas Chinese. Another dialect spoken by most overseas Chinese is Yue (Cantonese), which is spoken throughout central and southwestern Guangdong and the southeastern part of Guangxi province.

The written form of all Chinese dialects is the same. So while it is impossible for a Northerner to communicate in dialect to a Southerner, they will understand each other's written form perfectly.

Tête-à-tête—Chinese from different regions speak different dialects which are mutually unintelligible. However, they share a common script (*opposite*).

The language of instruction in Chinese schools is Putonghua, a northern Chinese dialect also known as Mandarin.

PUTONGHUA

Fortunately, China is united by a common tongue—Putonghua, or common language. It is also known as Mandarin. Putonghua is based on the Beijing dialect, which is a variation of the northern dialect, and since 1949, has been taught in schools across China. The Chinese language is the oldest continuously used language in the world today. It also has more speakers than any other language in the world.

Spoken Chinese has a limited range of sounds. There are only 400 sounds and 40,000 to 50,000 Chinese words. However, the limited number of sounds is made up for by variation in tones. There are four tones in Putonghua.

The four tones used to distinguish words from each other are:

1) high and level (as in *High* Noon)

2) rising (as in asking "*Here?*")

3) falling and rising (as in *re*quest)

4) low and falling (as in exclaiming "*No!*" in an argument)

So a word said in a different tone can mean something totally different:

"*Ni you bing* [first tone] *ma?*" – Do you have some ice?

"*Ni you bing* [third tone] *ma?*" – Do you have a cookie?

"*Ni you bing* [fourth tone] *ma?*" – Are you ill?

One has to be careful when asking for ice in a restaurant.

MINORITY LANGUAGES

The 55 minorities of China, some of which are broken into sub-groups, speak their own languages. The four main minority language groups are Altaic, Tibeto-Burmese, Tai and Miao-Yao.

The Altaic language group includes the Turkic languages spoken by the Uygurs and Kazakhs in Xinjiang and the dialects spoken by the Mongolians in Inner Mongolia. The Tibetans, Yi and Tujia minorities, who live mainly in the west and southwest, speak Tibeto-Burmese languages. Hill people who live in southern Sichuan and certain parts of Yunnan also speak Tibeto-Burmese languages. The Tai language group is spoken by a large number of minorities in Guangxi, Yunnan and Guizhou. The Miao and Yao languages are closely related to each other and belong to the Sino-Tibetan family.

After Liberation, institutes specializing in the research and development of minority languages were set up. One of their aims was to help minorities develop their own written script on the basis of the Latin alphabet.

Lessons for minority children are conducted in Putonghua, but the school curriculum also includes lessons in their mother tongue. Minority languages are used locally in books, newspapers and magazines. Radio and television programs in major minority languages such as Mongolian, Tibetan, Uygur, Kazakh and Korean are aired daily.

Nu women dressed in their best clothes, on their way to celebrate the Torch Festival. The Nus who live in Yunnan province speak a language belonging to the Tibeto-Burmese group, which has no written form. Few minority languages have their own script.

The development of Chinese words through the centuries. The top row of words are the sun, the second row the moon, third row vehicle and fourth row horse. The earliest known version is on left while on the right are words which have been in used since after A.D. 200.

THE WRITTEN LANGUAGE

There are over 50,000 Chinese words in the Chinese script of which only 3,000 are in common use. It is not surprising to know that not one person in Chinese history is known to know all the words. It is common practice for Chinese to reach for a dictionary to look up a word. They might do this because they have not seen the word before or they have forgotten how to write it.

Formed about 6,000 years ago, Chinese words are the oldest form of written language in the world. Chinese started expressing their ideas in drawings. Sometimes whole pictures were drawn and sometimes just the outline or representative part of an idea was used. They are known as ideographs. Take for example sun 日 , sheep 羊 , horse 马 .

In the early stages of its development, one ideograph represented one word. As more words were introduced, two or more ideographs combined to form new ideograms. For example, the ideograph for combine 合 and the ideograph for hand 手 together mean to take 拿 . Sometimes words express whole ideas; take for example *xiuxi* meaning "rest." There is a man 人 under a tree 木 resting his eyes 目 and his heart 心 — 休息 .

There are 11 basic strokes and Chinese words are written in a proper sequence. Written out of sequence, the word often loses its form and proportion. Children, when first learning how to write, practice for hours on what seems like totally unconnected dots, dashes and strokes. They soon learn how to decipher the sequence in which to write a word they see for the first time. The simplest word has only one stroke while the most complicated 30.

Chinese take their handwriting seriously as it reflects on their character and upbringing. Often, one's handwriting is a deciding factor in whether the letter is read or put aside for consideration. People of high standing

Che Che Cafe, or Vehicle Cafe, in Kunming. Che is the pinyin form of 车, meaning "vehicle."

often have very distinctive handwriting and are often privileged to put their handwriting on important signs or letterheads. There is even a restaurant in Beijing bearing a signboard in an emperor's handwriting because he stopped by one night and was impressed with the dumplings.

In 1964, the Chinese government introduced a form of simplified words on the mainland. These are made up of fewer strokes than the original word but keep the basic shape and meaning, for example the word bird—the original is 鳥, but is now written thus 鸟.

In an attempt to make Mandarin more intelligible to the Western world, a system known as *pinyin* was developed. The system translates phonetically Chinese words into Latin script.

BONE INSCRIPTIONS

In 1899, a Qing dynasty court official fell ill and sent for medicine from a pharmacy. What was prescribed were bone fossils. When his medication was brought to him, he noticed that the bones were engraved with Chinese words. He quickly ordered all the bones from the pharmacy to be brought to him to be examined. Scholars found that these bones, which were found by farmers and sold as medicine, dated back to the 16th to 11th century B.C. Over 1,500 words were recognized. The bone inscriptions explained why the sun, formally written as a dot within a circle, evolved into a square: because of the shape of the bones and simple carving tools used to inscribe words.

CHINESE IDIOMS

Chinese love their language. Their everyday conversation is sprinkled with idioms and puns. To use the correct idiom at the correct time is often appreciated and the person is looked upon as cultured or witty.

Most Chinese idioms consist of four words, though there are some with three, five or more words. Some of these idioms are fairly straightforward, for instance, "an old horse knows the road" (*lao ma shi tu*), but often, they do not make sense on their own unless one knows the story behind the saying. For example "to draw a snake and add feet to it" (*hua she tian zu*) describes someone who has already completed something and spoils it all by overdoing things. The story goes that there were some men who discovered a jar of wine which held enough only for one person to drink. They decided to hold a contest to see who could draw a snake in the sand. The fastest one got to drink the wine. The man who finished first had so much time to spare that he added feet to his snake. Then he snatched up the wine jar claiming it was his as he had finished first. The man who finished next claimed that although his friend had indeed finished first, there was no such thing as a snake with feet, so the wine rightfully belonged to him.

"Guarding the tree and waiting for the hare."

HOW TO COUNT TO TEN ON ONE HAND

The Chinese have a way of indicating the numbers one to 10 by the fingers of one hand. It is very useful at busy and noisy marketplaces where signing may be more effective than shouting the number of oranges one wants to buy.

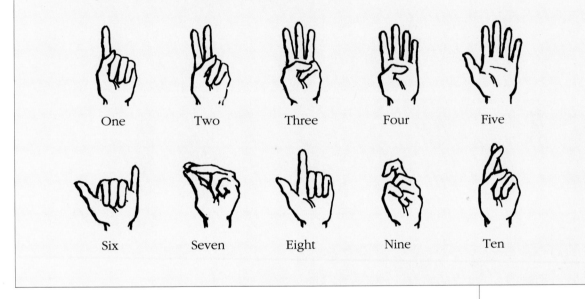

| One | Two | Three | Four | Five |

| Six | Seven | Eight | Nine | Ten |

"Guarding the tree and waiting for the hare" (*shou zhu dai tu*) describes a farmer who, in his greed, guards a secret that makes him look a fool. The farmer, who was on his way home, saw a hare running so fast that it crashed into a tree and broke its neck. The farmer happily had it for dinner that night, and the next day, went to the same spot to wait for another hare to do the same thing.

Another, "to pull the shoots to help it to grow" (*ba miao zhu zhang*), describes impatience. A farmer who planted some rice felt that his plants took a long time to grow, so he went out and started to pull the new shoots upward. Then he looked back with satisfaction at what he had done for the shoots were indeed taller. He went home to tell his family what he had done. His son rushed out and saw that the farmer's attempts left him not with a field of taller plants, but with a field of dead plants.

ARTS

MUCH OF ART STYLES of China developed in the Tang dynasty when artistic expressions reached a peak.

DECORATIVE ART

Chinese decorative art is distinctive. Symbols of nature, seasons and myths are included in the main designs of fabric, porcelain, ceramics and other Chinese handicrafts.

Round about the 7th century, a white clay was discovered along the banks of the Yellow and Yang Zi rivers. This clay produced white porcelain pieces that were later so refined that they were eggshell thin and translucent. Perhaps the most popular of these were the blue and white Ming porcelain pieces. They became so famous in the West that they were called "china," after their place of origin.

Another colorful form of art is cloisonné. Enamel paint, the most popular being blue, is used to fill in thin plates which are then soldered onto metal bases. Brought over from Persia during the Ming dynasty, cloisonné decorates everything from grandfather clocks to chopsticks.

The Chinese also refined the art of carving. Mostly done on jade or ivory, these pieces are sometimes so fine that special knives as small as toothpicks are used for the fine details.

An opera stage is quite bare and basic, sometimes with painted canvas backdrops representing a hall, garden or a palace. A small orchestra takes up one wing of the stage.

Previous pages: **A dough doll maker** (*page 80*). **Dough dolls are made of flour dough and last as long as the weather is cold. Ceramics for sale** (*page 81*).

OPERA

This classic Chinese form of entertainment started out as street performances where gongs, cymbals and drums were used to attract the audience. This "cacophony" is still the trademark of Chinese opera and marks the start of each new scene.

Each region of China has its own style of opera. Some stress singing, others acrobatics or dancing. Sung in the local dialects, they are still performed in the open.

The most popular style of Chinese opera comes from Beijing. Beijing opera started out 200 years ago in the capital. It took the best aspects of the different styles from other parts of China and integrated them into a style which includes singing, dancing, mime and acrobatics.

Stories in the operas are from historical epics, folk legends, classical novels and fairy tales. Lines are sung in classical Chinese with lyrics flashed by the side of the stage so the audience can follow the story or sing along, which they often do. Accompanying music is provided by an orchestra made up of Chinese fiddles, flutes, wooden clappers, lutes, drums, cymbals and gongs.

THE MONKEY KING

The Monkey King, or Sun Wukong, is probably the best-loved character in Chinese opera. There are five or six hundred operas which revolve around his adventures and antics. Most of these stories are based on the novel *Journey to the West* written by Wu Cheng'en in the 16th century.

Sun Wukong, a celestial being, accompanies his master, a Buddhist monk, to India, in search of religious scriptures. Along the way he goes through all kinds of dangers and hardships and meets demons and evil beings from which he protects his master.

He is a clever, cunning and often disobedient character with a good heart. He is totally devoted to his master. Always up to mischief, his monkey-like antics amuses audiences of all ages. Most operas about Sun Wukong are filled with acrobatics. Somersaults, tumbles and falls make up most of the spectacular fighting scenes. Actors who play the Monkey King spend their whole career perfecting the art and are able to imitate the actions and characteristics of the monkey well.

Chinese literature, of which the operatic drama is a part, has a 3,000-year history and is one of the major literary heritages of the world. It has greatly influenced the literary traditions of other Asian countries, particularly Korea, Japan and Vietnam. These countries have also adopted the Chinese script as part of their written language.

An evening at the opera can be a three- or four-hour affair. Whole Chinese families turn up for performances and the atmosphere in the theater is rowdy and almost festive, with drinks and melon seeds passed round. Shouts of "*hao!*" meaning "good" punctuate solo performances or exciting combat scenes. Spectators who stand up and join in the chorus are sometimes as entertaining as the actors on stage. Chinese love the opera and often one finds old men walking in the streets with transistor radios stuck to their ears listening intently to an opera.

OPERA PARAPHERNALIA

There are four major roles in each opera. The *sheng* or male lead is either an older man or a military or civilian hero, who is almost always strong, handsome and intelligent. *Dan* characters are female leads who are dignified, virtuous women, younger women who are witty and charming or military heroines. The *jing*, or *dahualian* (big painted face), is a male actor with a painted face emphasizing his strength or social standing.

The *sheng*, or male lead, here a military hero (as indicated by the pheasant feather on his headdress) who is also a scholar (indicated by the water sleeves).

Chou, or *xiaohualian* (small painted face), is the clown. He lends comic relief to the more serious scenes. These lead players are often set apart by the costumes they wear or their stage makeup.

Often heavily embroidered, and in dazzling colors, opera costumes add life to a relatively bare stage. Military heroes wear padded armors and splendid headdresses with long pheasant feathers. Men and women wear fluid robes with long "water" sleeves with which they use to great effect in flirting, crying and in showing fear or anger.

Stage makeup is as fascinating as the costumes. According to the roles they play, actors color their faces. Red represents loyalty and uprightness, white is slyness and treachery and yellow craftiness or cleverness. Blue and green are reserved for characters like evil spirits which are fierce and wicked, while silver and gold color the faces of gods and fairies. Heroes and heroines usually have simple white and pink-based faces with exaggerated eye makeup. Regular theater-goers are able to identify characters by their makeup.

ACROBATICS

This performing art has been in China for 22 centuries. It started out as a means of livelihood for farmers during the winter months and developed into one of the most popular forms of entertainment in China and abroad. This explains why the props used are often household items like crockery and furniture.

These objects are often tossed in the air or piled precariously one on top of the other. Balancing acts on bicycles, piles of chairs or large urns are common and so are contortionist acts.

Acrobatic acts often include performing animals.

Acrobats are so popular that there are acrobatic troupes that represent towns or large associations like the army or railroad workers.

The props on stage are usually a table and two chairs and perhaps a painted canvas backdrop. The audience has to imagine scenes in which one flag carried by a soldier represents a thousand men, two flags with wheels painted on them are a chariot and a flag with appropriate characters written on it may indicate a flood or strong winds. Actors who jump off chairs are trying to drown themselves in rivers or wells while actors climbing tables and chairs cross hills and mountain ranges.

Training for the opera is rigorous and actors start from as young as 10 years old.

Calligraphy on stone by Wang Xizhi, representing the earliest evolution of the "regular script," or *kai shu*.

CALLIGRAPHY

Chinese calligraphy is more than handwriting—it is an art. A well-written piece plays on the five senses, with the strokes conjuring up images of strength, beauty or grace. Sometimes one does not need to know what the characters mean as a piece can look graceful and feminine or strong and masculine, even vigorous, forceful, hot or cold. Calligraphers write poems, couplets or proverbs, which are hung on walls.

Chinese place great importance in good calligraphy and from the Tang to the Qing dynasty a scholar's handwriting carried great weight in his score at the civil service examination. A poet will take as much pride in the writing as in the content of his poems.

There are several forms of calligraphy. One is a formal style with regular characters which are angular, with no circles and few curved lines. Then there is the *chao shu,* or grass style, thus named because writing in this style appears as if the wind has blown over the grass. Only those who have studied calligraphy for a long time can decipher words written in this style. Another style is the *kai shu*, developed 2,000 years ago but still used by the Chinese today as regular writing.

The tools for Chinese calligraphy are few—brush, ink stick, ink stone and paper (sometimes silk), known as the four treasures of the study.

PAINTING

Chinese painting revolves around five subjects: human figures, landscapes, flowers, birds and animals, and fish and insects. Paintings are usually done on silk or an absorbent paper made of bamboo pulp. A pointed

A painter at work. The bamboo is one of four plants which make up one branch of Chinese painting. The other three plants are the orchid, the plum and the chrysanthemum. The bamboo symbolizes the unyielding integrity of a moral character.

brush is used to apply paint made of mineral and plant pigments. Color, if at all used, is applied in small amounts for a washed look.

Chinese paintings strive to catch the spirit of the subject. Artists sometimes meditate before picking up a brush and in a burst of energy put an image on paper. Works are painted from memory and executed quickly and confidently. Unlike Western art, a picture is completed in a matter of minutes and an artist paints the same subject again and again until he achieves the effect he wants. Many famous artists specialize in painting just one subject, such as birds, insects, shrimps or even donkeys.

Brush strokes are important to a painting and critics look out for how they contribute to the texture of a painting. They are given fancy names like "rain drops," "ax cuts," or "wrinkles on a devil's face." Calligraphy is almost always used to complete a Chinese painting. A couplet or poem complements the picture.

Finger painting started in the Tang dynasty and is regarded as a high art form. The fingernails are the main tools. They are kept long and well shaped as a broken nail hinders the artist.

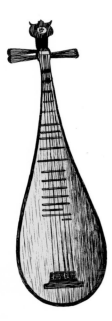

MUSICAL INSTRUMENTS

During his reign when Emperor Qin Shihuang burned all books, he burned most of the Chinese musical instruments as well. Most of what we see today are tribal instruments that have been adapted or adopted by the Hans to make Chinese music. Below are some of the instruments found in a Chinese orchestra.

ERHU This is a fiddle with two strings and played with a bow made of bamboo and horse hair. The *erhu* usually has a cylindrical sound box made of wood or bamboo. Animal hide such as sheep or snake skin is stretched over one of its sides creating different qualities of sound. Some of these fiddles are made of simpler materials such as coconut shells.

PIPA This a lute with four strings. It is held upright and its strings can be strummed or plucked. The *pipa* is a popular instrument in the towns along the Yang Zi River. Entertainers in tea houses strum their instruments while telling stories or singing.

Top right: **Guzheng**
Top: **Pipa**
Above: **Erhu**

GUZHENG This is a large zither with 18 to 21 strings. It is played like a horizontal harp and sounds almost like one. In ancient times, playing the *guzheng* was considered a status symbol—to be able to play it was to be cultured.

ARCHITECTURE

Chinese buildings have distinctive roofs and structures that set them apart from other buildings in the world. They are constructed from a series of vertical wooden pillars that increase gradually in height, thus giving the roof its unique shape.

Chinese buildings are built in clusters. These courtyard styled houses have buildings on each side of a square with inter-connecting halls. The main house faces south so that it is warm in winter and cool in summer. In the old days, the head of the household lived here, while the servants and children lived in the side houses.

Temples and palaces have similar layouts. They are more elaborately built with more courtyards lying side by side or one behind the other.

One of the most charming aspects of Chinese buildings is their elaborate ornamentation. Beams are often of red lacquer with designs of flowers painted on them while figures of animals and human beings sit on top of glazed tiles. Palaces are even more splendidly decorated with paintings of dragons and auspicious flowers and plants decorating ceilings, pillars and walls. Doors of palaces are always painted red for good luck and have rows of nine gold studs running vertically and horizontally. The Chinese believe this is the best number as it means a person is still in existence and still achieving. To reach 10 is to be at the end of the line and no Chinese wants that.

Red lacquered pillars and decorated beams of a covered walkway built in the traditional style.

PAPERCUTS

Papercuts are usually done by women in the countryside in their free time. The materials are simple: a piece of paper and a pair of scissors. One's imagination is used to snip randomly or precisely at the paper. Patterns can be regular, symmetrical repeated patterns or complicated designs with birds, animals, flowers or popular opera characters. Some can even depict a scene in life.

Papercuts are often used to decorate the house during festive seasons like the Spring Festival. Usually stuck on lanterns, windows, doors and walls, papercuts often have designs of flowers or symbols of good luck, longevity and health. Papercuts with the double happiness character are used during weddings to adorn gifts and sacrificial offerings, on wedding dowries, candlesticks and incense burners. Papercuts are also used as stencils for embroidery or indigo prints that go on clothes, bed linen or curtains.

Designs of papercuts are often handed down from generation to generation and designs differ from village to village. The appeal of this art form lies in its simplicity. It can be picked up and put down at any time.

The excitement of undoing a papercut lies in the fact that one never knows what to expect from a piece. Each piece is an original in itself.

EMBROIDERY

Embroidery was refined to an art form by women who wanted to wear something more than plain cloth. In the old days, a girl's embroidery skill (or lack of it) would indicate whether she would make a good wife or not.

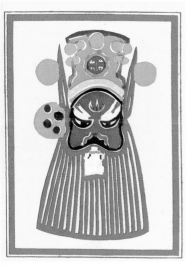

Papercuts of an opera figure (*top*) and a scene in history (*above*). Putting children and old folk at the city gate to confuse attacking enemies.

90

An embroidery of a landscape, not unlike a Chinese landscape painting.

Embroidery was first used with the discovery of silk thread. Embroidery decorates clothes, shoes, fans, purses and hair accessories. Motifs are different for men and women. Flowers, butterflies, geometric designs and phoenixes decorate women's clothes and accessories, while dragons and bold solid designs are considered masculine.

Embroidery is also used to decorate altar cloths, flags, banners and wall hangings. Designs on these are often of calligraphic characters, scenes of nature or people and animals.

Elaborate pieces of embroidery can take years to do and are often worked on by more than one person. Suzhou, Hunan, Sichuan and Guangdong are the embroidery centers of China. These regions have their own designs and styles. One of the most famous is the double-sided embroidery where the same image or sometimes a different one appears on the reverse side. The stitches of some pieces of embroidery are so fine that it is hard to tell one stitch from the next, and they look like paintings.

LEISURE

PARKS IN URBAN CHINA are seldom empty. As early as five every morning, the parks fill up with people. The majority of them are the elderly who start their day with a session of *taijiquan* or *qigong*, both martial art forms. Many believe this is the best time as *qi* (energy or force) can be drawn from nature into the body to replenish and invigorate one's own *qi*.

These exercises are usually done en masse with no particular leader. People will join whoever is in motion and sometimes half the park is filled with strangers united in exercise. In the summer months people sometimes switch to doing aerobics but this has a smaller following.

Parks are also filled with the songs of birds. These are the only pets city folk are allowed to have. The most popular of these birds is the Chinese thrush. Kept in round, beautifully carved cages often covered with blue cloth, these pampered pets love it when their masters swing their cages as they are walked to the park. Their cages are hung from the branches of trees while the birds compete loudly with one another.

Sundays will see groups of opera lovers and musicians gathering together in the parks to give impromptu performances. It can start with a man playing a fiddle while a passer-by bursts into song. Then another will join in. When everything is over, each goes their separate way and may never perform together again.

Parks on Sundays, like parks everywhere, see groups of families taking walks. The Chinese love posing for and taking photographs. Often, they pose with flowers, plants, statues and whatever they think will make a good picture. Sometimes people wait in line for a photograph of a commemorative statue or display.

Above: **A favorite pastime among the Chinese is keeping song birds which they take to the park, to compete with other birds.**

Opposite: **An *erhu* player in the park. Musicians like him attract other musicians and singers and impromptu performances are given.**

93

Right: **Parents with their children in the park.**

Below: **Tujia girls playing with stilts. Each girl is trying to force the other off her stilts.**

GAMES CHILDREN PLAY

Children in China play almost the same games as children around the world. Games such as hopscotch, jump rope, marbles and cat's cradle are all popular schoolyard games while computer games are everyone's favorite.

Boys also play a game with a heavy-based shuttlecock. They stand in a circle kicking the shuttlecock around trying to keep it up. There is another game boys play with a ball. One boy stands in the middle of a circle and tosses the ball high into the air and shouts the name of a friend. The named person must catch the ball, go into the circle and repeat the process. The person who fails to catch the ball or come to the center when his name is called is hit with the ball. This can be a painful and rowdy game but is lots of fun.

Girls like to play with a thick rope made of rubber bands. It is like a

THE STORYTELLER

The Chinese storyteller performs to audiences of all ages. He or she entertains with epics, classics, martial arts stories and contemporary stories. Often, his props, if any, are simple. It may only be a fan or a table and chair. The fan makes a wide sweep and tells of soldiers thundering across the desert. It then becomes a coy lady's accessory, or it could be slapped against the body to show the tyranny of an emperor.

The table, likewise, could become the front of a bus, a magistrate's table, a counter in a department store or a hospital bed. The magic lies in the storyteller's skill. Not only does he change the tone of his voice to become another person, but his expressions and behavior become that of a different person. The beauty of it all is the audience never mixes up the characters or train of events.

This profession started out with itinerant storytellers who moved from village to village providing entertainment. Some would light a joss stick and time it so that the most exciting part ended when the joss stick burned down. A hat was passed around and the story would continue. Audiences laughed, cried and trembled in fear with the storyteller.

Storytelling has become an art form and many variety shows on stage and on television include a storyteller. From this, another form of entertainment has evolved. Called crosstalk, it involves two or more people bouncing a comic script around like stand-up comics of the West.

large ring which is stretched between two girls while the rest take turns jumping in and out, twisting and turning, making patterns with the rope. The rope starts at the ankles of the two girls at either end and is raised higher and higher with each turn, making it more and more difficult.

Children in the countryside play simple games with whatever they can get their hands on. There is a game they play with pieces of paper the size of playing cards or, if that is not available, leaves. Each person has his share with one piece put in the center. The children then take turns trying to flip over the paper or leaf by slapping their own paper or leaf down near it. If the air current they produce succeeds in doing that, they get to keep the paper or leaf in the center.

An old man practicing *qigong*, a martial art said to prolong life.

MARTIAL ARTS

TAIJIQUAN Used by the Chinese since the 17th century, *taijiquan* is made up of hundreds of different positions originally used in self-defense. It is also known as "shadow boxing," for smooth, graceful, circular movements are combined with deep breathing and done with concentration. If *taijiquan* is correctly performed, one should break out in a light sweat. Perhaps the most beneficial feeling is that of calmness after the exercises.

Taijiquan has its origins in the preparation for combat. Controlled breathing and slow, circular body movements ensure that all the limbs and internal organs are exercised.

Taijiquan had only eight primary hand gestures and five body movements when it was first invented. More and more movements were added through the years and now there are five major styles of *taijiquan*. The more recently developed styles include quick movements with lively footwork and movements borrowed from fencing.

QIGONG This is a form of deep breathing exercise that aims to regulate the mind, body and breath. The aim of *qigong* is to achieve longevity. With breath control and concentration, *qi* can be directed to various parts of the body to increase strength and decrease pain. Some people use this skill to perform death-defying acts like lying under the wheels of a car or bending iron bars.

Most of the time, *qigong* is used as a therapeutic form of physical exercise, rather than for death-defying acts. It has been proven very useful in controlling various disorders such as high blood pressure, heart disease, aches and pains and breathing disorders. Therapeutic *qigong* can be done lying down, sitting, standing or walking. It stresses the calming of the mind and concentration and regulation of the breath. A combination of these stimulates the nervous system, increases blood circulation and metabolism and puts the body on the road to self-repair and self-renewal.

A *wushu* master giving a demonstration. *Wushu*, popularly known in the West as *kung fu*, is an art of self-defense, not attack.

WUSHU This art of fighting has been practiced for thousands of years not only as a form of self-defense, but as a form of physical exercise as well. There are four main categories of *wushu*: Chinese boxing with bare hands, duet boxing, sword play and group exercise.

The most popular form of *wushu* is Chinese boxing. This is what one would see in *kung fu* movies where hands and legs are used quicker than the blink of an eye and where jumps go on forever. There are many different forms of Chinese boxing. One form requires the use of strength while another cunning. The latter imitates the movements of 12 different birds and animals. The postures and movements of the dragon, tiger, monkey, horse, snake, eagle, sparrow, turtle and even the praying mantis are used.

Yet another form of Chinese boxing imitates drunkenness. "Eight Drunken Immortals" or the "drunken monkey" are regarded as high forms of *wushu*.

Weapons are sometimes used in *wushu* exercises. The saber, spear, sword, clubs and the nine-link chain are used against an armed or unarmed opponent.

Wushu aims to defend and not to attack. Students of this form of self-defense do it for the beauty and exercise of the art rather than for the purpose of fighting.

An improvised pingpong table. Pingpong is a favorite sport among the Chinese, and they play it anywhere, indoors and outdoors, on any surface which can bounce a pingpong ball.

SPORTS

All forms of sports are popular in China. Schools, factories and large organizations often have some form of sporting facilities like basketball courts, pingpong tables, badminton nets and rackets. Some organizations have 10 or 20 minutes a day put aside for mass exercises.

Pingpong, basketball and volleyball are the favorite sports of the Chinese. It is no wonder that they excel in them and produce some of the best international players. Seats to such games are seldom empty.

Pingpong played an important part in restoring diplomatic relations between China and the United States. In a move known later as "pingpong diplomacy," China invited a United States pingpong team to the country in 1971 and mended a 20-year rift.

In warmer weather, many Chinese disregard "no swimming" signs and take to rivers and canals for a swim. In winter, Northerners use the same rivers and canals for ice-skating.

CHINESE CHESS

In city park or quiet village square in the evening, there are men, seated on low stools, in deep concentration over a chessboard. They are playing elephant chess or *weiqi*, both strategy board games.

Elephant chess (see above) has been around since A.D. 700. Chess pieces include cannons, elephants, cavalry, infantry and chariots, with a fortress in which the king and his counselors are entrenched. The two halves of the chessboard are separated by the Yellow River. The objective is to storm the enemy's fortress and capture the king, who never leaves the fortress. Chessmen travel along lines, like in *weiqi*.

Weiqi, or "go," is the oldest board game in China, around for thousands of years. *Wei* means to surround while *qi* means board game. It is played with a grid board marked with 19 vertical and 19 horizontal lines and 181 black and 180 white flat, round counters. Players mark out their own territories and then try and capture each other's men and territory. Single or whole groups of men can be captured and removed from the board. The winner is the one who has gained the most territory and men.

Weiqi is considered the most complicated board game in the world because of the high number of possible moves.

FESTIVALS

THE CHINESE CALENDAR is basically an agricultural one which charts the changes of seasons, temperatures, rainfall and growing cycles. It follows the passage of the moon and divides the year into 12 lunar months. Because of this, it does not coincide with the Gregorian calendar. Chinese use the lunar calendar to mark their festivals and some of the older generation use the Chinese calendar more than the Western one because it marks the seasons more accurately. However, the Western calendar is adopted for daily use.

THE CHINESE ZODIAC

Legend has it that on his deathbed, the Buddha summoned all the animals of the kingdom to his bedside. Only 12 turned up and in order of their appearance, he dedicated a year to each of them. The Chinese zodiac moves in a cycle of 12 years and people born under these signs are said to possess certain characteristics.

rat	1960, 1972	– Charming, bright, creative and thrifty
ox	1961, 1973	– Steadfast, methodical and dependable
tiger	1962, 1974	– Dynamic, warm, sincere and a leader
rabbit	1963, 1975	– Humble, artistic and clearsighted
dragon	1964, 1976	– Flamboyant, imaginative and lucky
snake	1965, 1977	– Discreet, sensual, refined and intelligent
horse	1966, 1978	– Sociable, competitive and stubborn
sheep	1967, 1979	– Artistic, fastidious and indecisive
monkey	1968, 1980	– Witty, popular, versatile and good-humored
rooster	1969, 1981	– Aggressive, alert and a perfectionist
dog	1970, 1982	– Honest, conservative and sympathetic
pig	1971, 1983	– Caring, industrious and home-loving

Opposite: **Playing a game of riddles with lanterns during the Lantern Festival, on the 15th and last day of the Lunar New Year celebrations.**

MAJOR FESTIVALS

LUNAR NEW YEAR Falling on the first day of the first lunar month, this is the most important festival for Chinese in China and all around the world. It is usually between late January and late February, and marks the beginning of spring, so it is also known as the Spring Festival. As the year must begin with a good start, everything to ensure good fortune is done.

Preparations start with spring cleaning and decorating the home with symbols of good luck. New clothes are bought, rice bins are filled to the brim, larders are stocked, quarrels are mended and debts are paid.

The most important event of the New Year preparations is the reunion dinner. Children, no matter how far from home, make special efforts to be home with their parents on New Year's Eve. Certain foods are a must on the table. For example, in the North, *jiaozi* or dumplings are shaped like gold ingots which represent wealth.

At midnight on New Year's Eve, firecrackers are set off to scare away

Lion dances accompanied by cymbals, drums and gongs are a common sight during the Lunar New Year festivities. Celebrations for the New Year last for two weeks although most people are back at work by the fourth day. On the 15th day, a lantern festival marks the end of the celebrations.

any evil spirits. All lights in the house are turned on to chase away bad luck hidden in every corner. On the first day of the New Year, people dress in their new clothes to visit relatives. Children kneel and pay their respects to their elders. In return, they receive little red packets with money inside. Nothing unpleasant is allowed to happen on this day as it would represent things to come for the rest of the year.

QINGMING JIE The "clear and bright festival" comes around in early spring. This is the day the Chinese remember their dead ancestors. Visits are made to cemeteries to sweep their tombs clean and to pay their respects to them. This is not a solemn day as one would imagine. Burial grounds are usually in the countryside so visits to the cemetery are turned into family outings. Picnics are packed and activities such as kite-flying make these visits a festive affair.

DUANWU JIE This festival is held on the fifth day of the fifth lunar month and is known as the Dragon Boat Festival. It is held to remember a patriotic poet who drowned himself because his state was taken over by a neighboring state. Villagers rushed to the river and threw in rice dumplings to prevent the fish from eating his body. They spent days in their boats trying to recover his body and all they had to eat were rice dumplings filled with meat and wrapped in bamboo leaves. To remember this day, dragon boat races are held and rice dumplings are eaten.

ZHONGQIU JIE The 15th day of the eighth lunar month marks the time when the moon is at its fullest and brightest. This is when the Chinese celebrate the Mid-Autumn Festival. The autumn weather is at its best and people come out at night to admire the moon and enjoy the weather.

Chinese who are Taoist-Buddhist have altars and incense burners at home, either for ancestors or deities, or both. On the 1st and 15th of every lunar month, they burn joss sticks for their ancestors and deities. The more devout keep a vegetarian diet on these days.

Mooncakes made of a thin pastry filled with sweet mashed lotus seeds are eaten and given as gifts. The night is also filled with lights from paper lanterns. Children are often busy looking out for the lady in the moon.

Legend has it that the lady, Chang Er, had a husband who was a tyrannical king. He had a potion which could make him immortal and fearing for her people, Chang Er stole the potion and drank it. She immediately flew to the moon where she remains until today.

MINORITY FESTIVALS

TIBETAN BATHING FESTIVAL Between late summer and early autumn when the Wild Rat star is sighted in Lhasa, Tibetans celebrate the Bathing Festival. The festival lasts for seven days until the star is out of sight. Legend has it that during an epidemic, the Goddess of Mercy, Guan Yin, sent down seven fairies with seven bottles of holy water to be put into the rivers, lakes and ponds of Tibet. That night, everyone in Tibet dreamed that a girl covered in sores bathed in a river and was immediately cured. The next morning, all the sick people rushed to bathe in the rivers and were cured.

Tibetans now celebrate the festival by bathing and washing their clothes in rivers. While clothes and sheets line the banks of rivers to dry, their owners are in a festive mood drinking barley wine and buttered tea.

DAI WATER SPLASHING FESTIVAL The Dai minority of Yunnan celebrate the second day of their New Year by splashing water on each

Nu Torch Festival, held in the night, during which men and women, dressed in their traditional costume, gather for torch games and songs and dances. The Yis have a similar torch festival during which men and women look for potential spouses.

other. This is done to shower blessings and to wish happiness. The more water, the more wishes. This often means bucketfuls and lots of fun. The elderly are spared from this. Ladles of water are poured down their back or drops of water from wet olive branches are sprinkled on their heads while good wishes are uttered.

PUBLIC HOLIDAYS

China has one of the fewest public holidays in the world. It starts with a day off on January 1 followed by three days for the Spring Festival. May 1, Labor Day, is also a holiday and so are the first two days of October to celebrate the National Day.

The National Day Parade at Changan Avenue is a spectacular sight as columns and columns of men and women representing various organizations march through it.

The National Day is one of the grandest public celebrations in China. Grand celebrations are held in Beijing at Tiananmen Square with mass formation dances, with elaborate fireworks displays often the highlight of the evening.

Should a public holiday fall near the beginning of the week, for example a Tuesday, Chinese prefer to work on Sunday and take Monday and Tuesday off at a stretch.

Some holidays are meant for only certain groups of people. March 8 is International Working Women's Day and Chinese women get half a day off work. International Children's Day on June 1 means no school and May 4 being Chinese Youth Day means half a day off for young people.

FOOD

THE DAILY ACTIVITY that gives the Chinese the most joy is eating. "*Chi le ma?*" ("Have you eaten yet?") often follows "*Ni hao*" ("hello," or "how are you"). Sometimes they do not even say hello but ask whether the other has had a meal.

Because of poverty, Chinese have developed unique styles of cooking. Stir frying food cut up into small, even pieces that cook quickly saves precious firewood while braising and simmering soups use the same fire to warm the house and add something to the dinner table. Poverty also drove the Chinese to make the best use of an animal. There is a recipe for every part, except its fur or feathers.

KITCHEN ESSENTIALS

Chinese cook their food on two burners, fueled by firewood in the country and gas in the city. The kitchen holds few fancy appliances, the most popular being the electric rice cooker. The most important utensils are the cleaver, wok, a soup ladle and a pair of chopsticks.

The Chinese cleaver is a heavy knife with a broad, rectangular blade. Kept razor-sharp, it can hack hard bones, mince, slice and shred meat and vegetables very finely. Its flat side is used to bruise ginger and garlic while the blunt edge tenderizes meat and knocks out live fish effectively. The end of the handle is also put to good use, to crush garlic and mash black beans.

The wok is an all purpose cooking utensil. The best woks are made of cast iron but it is common to find them in stainless steel, aluminium or a non-stick material. They are a perfect half sphere with two handles on the side. The wok can be used for deep fat frying, shallow frying, stir frying, boiling and simmering. Sometimes a pair of chopsticks is placed across the base and a plate or bowl balanced across to steam food.

Opposite: **The wedding feast, ready to go to the groom's home, as part of the bride's dowry.**

Below: **A kitchen must is the versatile wok, used to steam, fry, boil, braise and simmer food. It usually comes with a dome-shaped cover to catch the steam to cook food faster.**

LIBRARY
LYNDHURST HIGH SCHOOL
LYNDHURST, N. J.

RICE

Rice is so important to a Chinese that *fan* means both cooked rice and a meal. Many sayings revolve around rice. The bread winner is one who "puts rice on the table" while "to break one's rice bowl" means making another lose his job. A sick person "cannot eat rice" and a Chinese asking one to "come and eat rice" is inviting one to a meal.

Rice is treated with utmost respect. Every spilt grain is swept up, cleaned and cooked. Parents persuade their children to eat up every grain of rice in their bowl by telling them that a bowl dotted with rice grains means that they will marry someone with pock-marked skin. *Fan* is eaten with *cai*, a general term for dishes that accompany rice.

There are 7000 varieties of rice, all cooked and eaten in different ways. One of the most unusual rice recipes is "exploded rice." Uncooked rice is put into a drum which is heated over charcoal to a high temperature. It is churned and when the meter reaches a certain pressure a valve is released and, with a bang, the rice grains spill out into a waiting bag. The grains look and taste like rice crispies, and are eaten as a snack or pressed together with syrup to make a cookie.

CHOPSTICKS

Chinese started eating with chopsticks thousands of years ago. They were probably invented to pick up bite-sized pieces of food. Soldiers going to war had a special kit consisting of a cutting knife and a pair of chopsticks. Regular chopsticks are tapered, slim objects with a blunt end. They are about eight inches long, though those for cooking purposes are about two feet long.

Chopsticks are made of a variety of materials, the most common being wood, bamboo or plastic. The more elaborate ones have cloisonné designs or are made of ivory or jade. Emperors ate with silver chopsticks, believed to turn black if the food was poisoned.

Chinese use chopsticks to eat everything except soup. They are used to quickly push rice from the bowl into the mouth, pick up small pieces of food and even eat cake! Children start using them as soon as they can pick up a pair and coordinate their movements. There is no rule as to how they should be used, except that they should never cross. The aim is to get food into the mouth as quickly as possible.

REGIONAL CUISINE

BEIJING CUISINE This northern cuisine is characterized by the liberal use of garlic and chillies to whet the appetite. Food is often drenched in oil and seasoned with vinegar, salt and sugar. Less rice is eaten in the North as wheat grows better in the drier weather. Plain steamed buns or wheat pancakes are eaten as a staple, with stir-fried dishes of diced meat and vegetables or stewed meats. Wheat dumplings stuffed with minced meat and vegetables are eaten as a main meal especially in winter.

Beijing food also includes dishes from neighboring Mongolia. One of the most popular is skewered mutton. Sold along the streets, skewers of mutton are fried in oil and rolled in powdered chilli and cumin. Mongolian rinsed mutton is also popular. Diners sit around a charcoal-heated funneled pot, dipping thin slices of mutton into the hot water. The barely cooked meat is dipped into a sauce of fermented bean curd and eaten with similarly cooked Chinese cabbage and vermicelli.

Fish farming in Wuxi. Fish breeding has been in China for centuries. The long coastline of China provides large regions with abundant fish while rivers and lakes provide fresh water fish to landlocked provinces.

Chinese like to buy their fish fresh and, whenever possible, still alive and swimming. These are packed in water-filled bags for the customer.

The carp is most prized because it represents diligence, ambition, courage and determination.

SHANGHAI CUISINE   This covers the lower Yang Zi river delta. This region is known as the "Land of Rice and Fish," and its cuisine revolves around whatever can be caught in the rivers. Fish, eels and shrimps are steamed or cooked in tasty soy and sugar based sauces. Another favorite condiment is black vinegar which is used as a dip or in a sauce. Like northern cuisine, a lot of oil and chillies are used and the simple cooking methods bring out the best in the flavor of the food.

SICHUAN CUISINE   Sichuan food is the spiciest in China. Most dishes are covered in a red chilli oil and sprinkled with a potent, fragrant pepper. This pepper has a delayed numbing effect on the tongue that can deaden all sense of taste for several seconds. Fish is hard to find as the area sits on a basin with rapidly flowing rivers. To make up for this, pork, beef and eggplant are cooked in "fish flavored sauce" which is actually a

110

mixture of vinegar, hot bean paste, ginger, garlic and scallions.

Other Sichuan specialties include Camphor and Tea Smoked Duck where the fowl is slowly smoked over a fire of camphor chips and tea leaves. The fragrant duck is then deep fried and eaten with a thick sweet soy sauce. Dan Dan Noodles are also a favorite. Cold boiled noodles are tossed into a bowl and seasoned with chilli oil, ginger juice, garlic paste, soy sauce, vinegar and sugar. Sometimes, this is topped with shreds of cucumber and sesame seed paste.

A restaurant window in the town of Guanxian, Sichuan. Note the string of green chillies in the center. Sichuan food is well-known for its spiciness.

CANTONESE CUISINE This is the best known form of Chinese cuisine outside of China. The Cantonese are known to be very fussy about the freshness of the ingredients. Fish are usually swimming in tanks minutes before they are brought to the table in a soup or ginger sauce. Dishes are never overcooked and flavors are seldom masked with heavy or pungent sauces. Vegetables are lightly stir fried or blanched in hot water and dressed with oyster sauce. The Cantonese are also famous for their thin egg noodles which are eaten with a dumpling soup or topped with red-roasted meats. Soups are an integral part of Cantonese cuisine. Sometimes boiled with traditional Chinese herbs, these soups are simmered for hours over a charcoal fire and the rich, tasty soup is drunk as part of dinner.

CHINESE SNACKS

Chinese snacks are called *dian xin*. Translated, it means "to dot the heart." The portions of these snacks do just that. But with the variety of snacks, one can easily make a heavy meal of them. Snacks are an important part of life to a race that eats frequently at all times of the day.

Across China, vendors tend to huge bamboo steamers that hold *bao zi*, meat buns, or *shao mai*, little cup-shaped meat dumplings wrapped in a thin dough skin. Little bowls of noodles tossed in condiments or drenched in fish or beef soup are delicious. Huge woks of boiling oil are used to fry dough sticks called *you tiao*. Some people call them *youzhagui*, meaning "fried devils." The story goes that a general was so angry with his enemies that he made effigies of them in dough, which he fried and ate.

Sweet snacks usually come in the form of beans cooked in a light syrup served in bowls. Sometimes these beans are mashed and wrapped with a glutinous rice skin. Looking like perfect marbles, they are boiled and served in syrup. Nuts and seeds also make popular snacks. Peanuts are finely ground and cooked into a thick soup. It tastes like watered down peanut butter and is sometimes served as a dessert. Sesame seeds are sometimes cooked in the same way.

OODLES OF NOODLES

Noodles, or *mien* in Chinese, come in all shapes, sizes and lengths. In the North, they are made of plain wheat and water and look like flat spaghetti. They can be eaten plain, dressed in garlic, chillies and vinegar, boiled in a plain soup or fried with chives and soy sauce.

In western China, *shou mien*, or hand noodles, and *la mien*, pulled noodles, are more popular. Hand noodles are made with the same wheat-and-water dough. Bits of dough are plucked and thrown into boiling water. With pulled noodles, bits of dough are pulled into thick lengths before being boiled. Both these noodles are fried in a tomato based sauce with onions, bell peppers and bits of mutton.

In Shanxi province, cut noodles are a specialty. Lumps of dough are held in the hand and slices of it are cut into a boiling pot of water. Master noodle makers are so skilled that they balance lumps of dough on their hats while they slice off pieces with knives held in each hand.

In the South, egg is added to the wheat dough. Sometimes a few drops of alkaline water are added to give the noodles a slightly bitter, but not unpleasant, taste. Rice flour is also used to make noodles in the South. Noodles here are round or flat and can be as thick as spaghetti, or as fine as hair. They are fried plain or crispy, topped with a hearty sauce of shrimps and pork or added to a rich soup.

Long noodles symbolize a long life and are served at birthday celebrations.

Noodles drying in the sun. There is a debate as to who invented noodles. The Chinese claim that Marco Polo took the art of noodle-making from China to Italy while the Italians like to believe that he brought the skill of noodle making with him to China.

Opposite: **A street vendor selling *shaobing*, or sesame pancake, in Guilin, southwest China. Snacks are an important part of life to a race that eats frequently at all times of the day.**

Frog's legs fried in ginger and scallions are said to strengthen one's legs.

CHINESE EXOTICA

"If it moves and its back faces the sun, the Chinese will eat it." The Cantonese are especially famous for their exotic taste in meat. Snake is made into a thick soup while dog is roasted or stewed. Hard-to-find iguanas are preciously suspended in wine and taken in small amounts for their tonic effect. Chinese believe that the more exotic the meat is, the more tonic the effects on one's health. For example, dried pieces of crocodile meat made into a soup are said to do wonders for a child's cough.

Bears' paws are now hard to find, but when they do come by, they are lovingly braised and served to very important guests. Camels' hooves are more common. They are similarly prepared and have no particular taste and a gelatinous texture. Fortunately or unfortunately, the Chinese camel has two humps. Braised in stock, they look and taste like lumps of fat. Camels' noses are not spared either and, each camel having only one, they make a much rarer dish.

Other delicacies include bird's nests, that is, the dried mucus from a swallow's salivary glands that the bird uses to line its home. Served in sweet or savory soups, bird's nests are regarded as a delicacy and a tonic. Shark's fins are made into a rich, thick soup while sea slugs and jellyfish are prepared in a variety of ways.

Chinese also do strange things to ordinary food. "Century eggs" start as fresh ones covered in an alkaline ash and kept for a month or longer in a cool dark place. By that time, the egg white has turned into a black jelly and the yellow yolk is ringed with grey. This is often eaten as an appetizer with vinegar or pickled ginger.

FOOD TABOOS

It is hard to imagine the Chinese not eating something or other. Those who restrain themselves do so because of religion or because it upsets the *yin–yang*, or heat–cold, balance of the body.

Some Chinese do not eat beef. This is because they feel it not morally right to eat an animal that has worked so hard to put rice on their tables. The Chinese word for cow and buffalo are the same and, although it is the buffalo that has worked in the rice fields and on the farms, the cow escapes being eaten as well.

Moslems in China do not eat pork on religious grounds. All other meat they eat has to be slaughtered according to Islamic law.

Some Taoists do not eat meat at all. A few abstain for a lifetime while others on certain days of the year to cleanse the body and mind. Some Buddhists, too, are vegetarians. They abstain because it is their philosophy not to take any form of life. Vegetarians do not eat eggs, neither do they eat garlic, onions and ginger. They believe that these stimulate tempers and they may end up too passionate to attain peace.

Hairy crabs, a species of crabs found in the rivers of Shanghai during autumn, are never eaten with persimmons. The two are considered very *yin,* or cooling, and the combination could make one sick.

Pork, found in seven out of 10 Chinese meat recipes, is taboo to the Moslems.

When Chinese eat out, the decor of the restaurant is often the least important factor. Most Chinese restaurants are simply furnished with bare essentials.

Banquet tables, complete with plates of snacks, ready for the guests.

BANQUETS

Chinese banquets are noisy, long meals which leave one so full that one could skip two meals. It starts with nibbles like peanuts, candied walnuts or pickled cabbage to keep the diners busy before the meal starts. Sometimes, cold cuts will be sitting on the table before the guests arrive.

There are usually 10 guests at each round table. At each setting is a

THE TEN COURSE DUCK DINNER

You will never know how many ways to eat a duck or how many parts of a duck could be eaten till you've had a full Peking Duck dinner.

The first course is made up of a cold platter with various cuts of duck, gizzard, liver and ducks' tongues usually cooked in a dark soy sauce. Duck's webs and brains are included.

The *piece de resistance* is the skin of the duck which has been roasted to perfection. Pieces of the skin are carved out with a cleaver, dipped in a sweet-salty soy sauce and wrapped in a pancake made of flour and lard. The meat of the duck is then stir fried with noodles, the wings are braised, bits of it are fried with a variety of vegetables and finally, the bones are made into a clear soup.

You will be pleased to know that the dessert does not include duck in any form. But if you're interested in eel, there is a restaurant in Beijing that has a 10-course eel dinner which includes a dessert made of the fish.

small saucer for soy sauce, a plate, a small bowl, a pair of chopsticks, a spoon and some glasses for soft drinks and spirits.

Dinner starts with hors d'oeuvres which are a mixture of a few hot and cold food such as seasoned jellyfish and century eggs. The platter is often elaborately decorated with the food making geometric designs or forming part of a peacock's tail. Guests usually help themselves and the host will always make sure that their plate is constantly full.

Dishes are served one at a time, to be admired before being consumed. There are usually 10 dishes at a banquet. The second last dish is usually a soup to wash everything down followed by fried rice or noodles to "fill the stomach" just in case one did not have enough.

Dessert at the end is sometimes some sort of flaky pastry filled with mashed beans or nuts or a sweet soup with whole beans or nuts and a fruit platter.

The best of Chinese banquets is the emperor's banquet which consists of 132 courses, all at one sitting. No wonder the Chinese equivalent for *bon appetit* is *man man chi*, please eat slowly.

Fresh food market in Wuhan. What a region produces determines what one puts into the cooking pot.

HOME COOKED MEALS

Chinese are particular about the freshness of their food. If they have the time, shopping for fresh vegetables is a daily affair. What they buy will be whatever is in season. In the North, for example, winter means almost daily meals of Chinese cabbage. This hardy vegetable is grown in autumn and survives the bitterly cold winter. Outer leaves are removed to reveal fresh, crispy leaves within.

Breakfast is usually rice gruel made from leftover rice or broken pieces of grains too small to make a good pot of rice. It is eaten with a variety of pickled vegetables or pieces of salty fermented bean curd. In the South, pieces of meat and an egg is added to the gruel to make a tasty congee. Fried dough sticks, unleavened bread sprinkled with sesame seeds or noodles are sometimes eaten.

Dinner is the main meal of the day and is eaten early, between 5 and 6 p.m. Family members sit around a table filled with all the dishes for dinner. The soup usually sits in the middle, surrounded by two or three dishes of vegetables and a main dish of fish, poultry or pork. Family members have a bowl of rice each, and help themselves to whatever they want from the common dishes.

Chinese cooking is a balance of contrasting tastes and textures. There will never be two sweet-sour dishes served together nor will they think of having two deep-fried dishes on the same table. Soups are served as part of a meal and are used to cleanse and refresh the palate during the meal.

TABLE MANNERS

Do not be surprised if a Chinese eats noisily at the table. It is not considered bad manners to slurp soup although it is poor upbringing if one chews noisily. To use chopsticks as drumsticks on the table is disrespectful. Chopsticks are also never used to point at a person or gesticulate during a conversation.

Sitting down to a meal together.

A meal only starts when everyone is seated. Children will invite their elders to eat before starting their own meals. Usually, a mouthful of plain rice is eaten first before any of the other dishes are touched. A person first helps himself or herself to the nearest dish. Food taken from any dish must be from the part of the plate nearest the person. Morsels of food must be taken from the top. It is rude to flip over pieces of food or take pieces from the bottom of the plate. A person also never goes for the best pieces, which are offered to the oldest person at the table or the guest.

Chinese think it is perfectly all right to put bones on the table. In some local restaurants, bones are even deposited on the floor.

WHAT'S IN A NAME?

Chinese get very poetic about the names of their dishes. Reading a menu is sometimes like reading a fairy tale as sometimes no food is mentioned, only phoenixes, jade stalks and lion's heads. Spinach served with boiled bean curd is known as Red-Beaked Green Parrots on White Marble while a Lion's Head is a meatball the size of a baseball.

Ants Crawling Up A Tree Trunk is less dangerous than one may think. It is only ground meat cooked with transparent bean vermicelli. Pock Marked Bean Curd sounds unappetizing but is named after a woman with unfortunate skin, who invented the dish of bean curd cooked with minced meat and hot broad bean paste. The white pieces of bean curd swimming in a sauce red with chilli oil and bits of minced pork does look like a skin problem.

Red-Cooked Water Paddles are quite tasty, being fish fins cooked in a soybean sauce. Drunken Chicken is cold chicken marinated in wine while Beggar's Chicken has a more colorful background. A beggar once stole a chicken and, afraid of being found out, coated it with mud, feathers and all, and threw it into his fire. When the coast was clear, he cracked the hardened mud and the chicken was fragrant and delicious.

Monk Jumps Over The Wall is one of the most expensive dishes one could order. It is made up of all sorts of dried seafood stewed slowly in a clay pot. The story goes that a meditating monk was distracted by a wonderful aroma wafting over from the other side of the wall. After a while, he could not stand it any longer and decided to jump over and ask for a bowl, hence the name.

The chicken is not chicken on a Chinese menu, but rather the more fanciful "phoenix."

WINE

Chinese wines are made from rice, sorghum, millet or grapes which are naturally fermented. The most popular wines are made from rice. There are three main types of wine, white wine, yellow wine and burning wine, which are spirits. White wine is made from glutinous rice and is light and sweet. Yellow wine is also made from rice. It has a much stronger flavor and turns darker with age. Chinese spirits are potent, often colorless liquids which have a very high alcohol content that can make one's mouth and stomach seem on fire. Chinese like to drink their wine warmed and in small cups, which they empty in one gulp.

There are many stories about Chinese wine. One of the most famous Chinese poets, Li Bai, is said to have written his best pieces while intoxicated. Many of his poems speak of the joys of wine and the wonderful companion it makes. He is believed to have drowned trying to rescue the moon, which he in a drunken state thought had fallen in the lake.

Another tale tells of an emperor's forgotten pot of rice which fermented into wine. It tasted so good that there was a tasting party which left everyone with a hangover. The emperor decreed that wine should always be drunk from tiny cups, that it must always be taken with food, and that mild mental or physical exercise should be done when drinking wine.

In Shaoxing, famous for its yellow wine, a father seals and buries an earthen jar of good wine the day his daughter is born. This wine is unearthed when the girl marries and is used as part of her wedding celebrations.

Wine fermenting in a cellar. One of the most famous Chinese wines is Maotai, a transparent, potent spirit made from sorghum.

TEA

A teahouse in Sichuan. Tea-drinking has been a habit among the Chinese for thousands of years, as revealed by literary references from as early as A.D. 270. It is said that a few leaves of the camellia accidentally fell into an ancient sage's pot of boiling water. He found the brew pleasant and repeated the experiment. Thus, tea was born.

Tea is the most important beverage in all parts of China. It is drunk instead of water at all times of the day. In ancient China, it was used for medicinal purposes and the modern Chinese still swear by it. They believe it stimulates the digestive system, nervous system and heart, reduces the harmful effects of smoking and alcohol and cuts fat.

Most of China's tea grows in the South. The finest are found growing on mist covered cliffs so high up that trained monkeys are used to pluck them. There are basically three types of tea: green, red and oolong ("black dragon") tea. Green tea is made from dried young tea leaves which make a light refreshing drink. Red tea is made from leaves that have been fermented and toasted, making a stronger, more flavorful tea. Oolong tea is made from partially fermented leaves and is the most widely drunk tea in China and abroad. Sometimes jasmine flowers are added in the fermentation process of green or oolong tea to perfume it.

THINGS YOU DIDN'T KNOW ABOUT TEA

- On formal occasions, tea is served in a covered teacup which sits on a saucer. Leaves are left in the cup to leach and the tea is drunk with the cover on to strain the tea leaves.
- When one's cup is refilled with water, it is the norm to rap one's knuckles on the table three times to indicate thanks. This gesture was started by court officials who accompanied a Qing emperor traveling incognito. When he refilled their tea cups, they rapped thrice, representing the kowtows of thanks they could not perform.
- There are 30 types of tea in the world and they are all found growing in Yunnan province.
- The frugal Chinese never throw away their used tea leaves. Some leave them on a saucer in a cupboard to absorb unpleasant smells. Others dry them in the sun and use them to make light and cool pillows.
- Tea is also used in the kitchen to smoke meat or boiled with soy sauce and eggs to make delicately flavored "tea eggs."

- Chinese porcelain was shipped to the West in wooden crates filled with tea as a shock absorber. Both were sold at exorbitant prices.
- Chinese drink their tea without milk or sugar. Tea is considered *yin*, or cooling, and the old Chinese will shake their heads at the idea of drinking iced-tea.
- A marriage is recognized when tea served by the bride is formally accepted by the bride's parents-in-law.
- Garlic breath from a Chinese meal can be eliminated by chewing the tea leaves from one's cup. The chlorophyll in the leaves will freshen breath.

Everyday tea is made by the mugful by adding hot water to a spoonful of tea leaves that last the whole day. Or, it can be made in teapots. The water should just come to a boil, then be poured into a warmed teapot holding the tea leaves. It is allowed to stand for three to five minutes and drunk from porcelain cups. Tea connoisseurs make their tea in tiny brown clay teapots that hold about a tablespoon of tea leaves. Hot water is added to the leaves and thrown away. The second addition of hot water brings out the flavor of the tea.

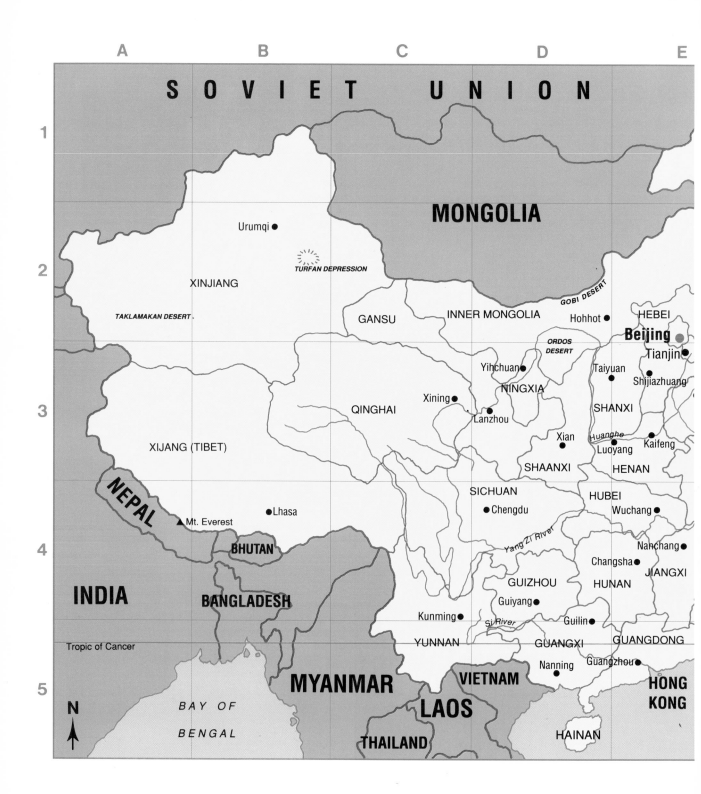

F **G**

HEILONGJIANG

● Harbin

● Changchun

JILIN

● Shenyang

LIAONING

SEA OF
JAPAN

KOREA

SHANDONG
● Jinan

YELLOW
SEA

Grand Canal

JIANGSU

JAPAN

EAST
CHINA
SEA

Hefei ● Nanjing
●

● **Shanghai**

ANHUI

● Hangzhou

ZHEJIANG

Fuzhou ●

FUJIAN

PHILIPPINE

SEA

TAIWAN

CHINA

Anhui E4

Beijing E2

Fujian E4

Gansu C2
Gobi Desert D2
Grand Canal E3
Guangdong E5
Guangxi D5
Guangzhou E5
Guizhou D4

Hainan D5
Hebei E2
Heilongjiang F1
Henan E3
Hubei E4
Hunan E4
Huanghe E3

Inner Mongolia D2

Jiangsu E3
Jiangxi E4
Jilin F2

Liaoning F2

Mt. Everest A4

Ningxia D3

Qinghai C3

Shaanxi D3
Shandong E3
Shanghai F4
Shanxi E3
Si River D5
Sichuan D4

Taklamakan Desert A2
Tianjin E3
Turfan Depression B2

Xian D3
Xijang (Tibet) B3

Yunnan C5
Yang Zi River D4

Zhejiang E4

───── **International Boundary**
───── **Provincial Boundary**
───── **Tropic of Cancer**
▲ **Mountain**
● **Capital**
● **City**
〜 **River**

QUICK NOTES

LAND AREA
3.7 million square miles

POPULATION
1.2 billion

PROVINCES
Hebei, Shanxi, Liaoning, Jilin, Heilongjiang, Shaanxi, Gansu, Qinghai, Shandong, Jiangsu, Zhejiang, Anhui, Jiangxi, Fujian, Taiwan, Henan, Hubei, Hunan, Guangdong, Hainan, Sichuan, Guizhou, Yunnan

AUTONOMOUS REGIONS
Inner Mongolia, Ningxia, Xinjiang, Guangxi, Tibet

MUNICIPALITIES
Beijing, Shanghai, Tianjin

MAJOR RIVERS
Yang Zi River, Huanghe, Si River

MAJOR DESERTS
Taklamakan, Gobi

HIGHEST POINT
Mt. Qomolangma (Mt. Everest, 29,089 feet)

NATIONAL LANGUAGE
Putonghua (Mandarin)

MAJOR RELIGIONS
Taoism, Confucianism, Buddhism, Islam, Christianity

CURRENCY
Renminbi Yuan (U.S.$1 = Y5.2)

MAIN EXPORTS
cotton, coal, crude and refined oil, cement, rolled steel

IMPORTANT ANNIVERSARIES
Anniversary of the founding of the People's Republic of China (October 1), Anniversary of the founding of the Communist Party of China (July 1), People's Liberation Army Day (August 1)

LEADERS IN POLITICS
Sun Yat-sen (founder of Modern China), Mao Zedong (founder of Communist China), Deng Xiaoping (paramount leader)

LEADERS IN LITERATURE
Lao She (writer), Ba Jin (writer), Lu Xun (writer), Guo Moruo (writer)

GLOSSARY

bao zi	Steamed buns with minced meat filling.
danwei	Work units which look after workers (and their families) from the time they start working until the time they die.
Guan Yin	Chinese Goddess of Mercy.
jiaozi	Crescent-shaped dumplings filled with meat and vegetables.
qi	Energy or force that flows through all living things.
qigong	Martial art practiced as a form of therapeutic exercise.
taijiquan	Chinese shadow boxing.
weiqi	Chinese board game played with black and white markers.
wushu	Chinese martial arts.
yang	The active life force or energy.
yin	The passive life force or energy.

BIBLIOGRAPHY

Carter, Alden: *Modern China*, Franklin Watts, New York, 1986.
Minford, John (translator): *Favourite Folktales of China*, New World Press, Beijing, 1983.
Miyazima, Yashukiko: *Children of the World: China*, Gareth Stevens, Milwaukee, WI, 1988.
Rau, Margaret: *Holding up the Sky: Young People in China*, Lodestar Books, New York, 1983.
Wei Jinzhi: *100 Allegorical Tales from Traditional China*, Joint Publications, Hong Kong, 1982.
Wood, Frances: *People at Work in China*, David and Charles, New York, 1988.

INDEX

PICTURE CREDITS
Bernard Sonneville: 11, 12, 18, 23, 25, 27, 29, 32, 40, 41, 43, 51, 52, 56, 62, 63 (box), 67, 74, 84, 85, 88, 94, 97, 108, 110, 117, 118
Wang Miao: 1, 8–10, 13, 15, 28, 34, 32, 33, 55, 58, 60, 68, 69, 75, 80–82, 89, 93, 100, 102, 104, 105, 116, 119, 122
Liz Berryman: 4, 7, 14, 36–38, 49, 54, 61, 72, 77, 98, 99, 107, 111, 112
Chapman Lee: 26, 30, 59, 66, 70, 73, 86, 87, 91, 106, 121, 123
Life File: 5, 20, 50, 113, 114
Jimmy Kang: 16, 35, 39, 92
Peggy Ferroa: 31, 57, 115
Ed Stokes: 42, 96
Lawrence Lim: 63 (bottom right)
Yim Chee Peng: 120

DATE DUE

951
FER
92-12

Ferroa, Peggy
China

DATE DUE	BORROWER'S NAME
2/04/02	

951
FER
Ferroa, Peggy
China

LIBRARY
LYNOHURST HIGH SCHOOL